SOME
TRINIDAD
YESTERDAYS

P.E.T. O'CONNOR

DEDICATION

To my children, the fruits of my yesterdays

CONTENTS

Preface to this edition   6

CHAPTER 1   The Founding Fathers   7

CHAPTER 2   The Social Structure   14

CHAPTER 3   Enter the O'Connors   20

CHAPTER 4   Slavery   34

CHAPTER 5   The East Indians   42

CHAPTER 6   The Years after Emancipation   46

CHAPTER 7   My Generation: Boyhood Days   55

CHAPTER 8   On Donkeys, Mules and Horses   67

CHAPTER 9   A Visit to Port of Spain   77

CHAPTER 10 Schooling   81

CHAPTER 11 La Chance   83

CHAPTER 12 The Oil Age   91

CHAPTER 13 The Post-war Years   101

CHAPTER 14   The Oilfields of the Twenties   106

CHAPTER 15   1937   117

CHAPTER 16   The War Years (and after)   124

Appendix   131

About the author   135

PREFACE TO THIS EDITION

MY father's book went out of print several years ago. But it is still sought after by family, friends, and those who want to know more about the story of Trinidad. With the permission of Inprint Caribbean, the original publisher, I have produced this edition.

It has been a great pleasure, and a most revealing exercise, to read again the story of the O'Connor family in Trinidad, and the historical context in which it was set. I was reminded of an incident, shortly before independence, when I had recently been commissioned into the Royal Air Force. I had managed to join an RAF contingent that was deployed to Piarco. The Country Club put on a cocktail party to entertain the visitors. At the party I was talking to a black man, when Dad took me aside and said: "You shouldn't be talking to him. He's a black fellow". In those days the only "black fellows" present at the Country Club would have been servants. I explained to Dad that he was an RAF officer, senior to me, the navigator of the aircraft on which I had flown. Dad was fully apologetic, and soon afterwards he, like the rest of society, gracefully accepted the new racially relaxed nation that Trinidad had become. Readers will find this change admirably described in the book.

I hope that readers will find as much satisfaction and enjoyment in these pages as I have.

Patrick O'Connor
April 2023

CHAPTER 1

THE FOUNDING FATHERS

THE foundations of Trinidad's social structure were laid by Phillip Rose Roume de Saint-Laurent who visited the then Spanish colony in 1777. The island had been a Spanish colony for nearly 300 years, but Spain had done little or nothing with it. Entrenched in their capital at St. Joseph, the few Spanish families had cultivated the fertile valleys of Maracas and Santa Cruz but had ventured no further afield. Port of Spain had remained a small fishing village with a population of about 400, a "mixture of Indianised half-breed Spaniards and some full blooded French strangers."

It was at this stage that the island was rediscovered by Saint- Laurent. A member of one of the aristocratic French families who had helped to build the French empire in Louisiana and the Caribbean, Saint-Laurent had established himself as a prosperous planter in Grenada, but the prosperity of Grenada, like that of the other French colonies, was now on the wane. On hearing favourable reports of Trinidad, he came to see and was enchanted. He bought some land in Diego Martin and returned to Grenada to urge his countrymen to cast their lot in Trinidad. He then set off for Spain to petition the king to permit the French colonists and others free entry into the island.

As the direct result of Saint-Laurent's petition, the Spanish government issued its Cedula of Population in 1783 and the foundations of a new nation were laid. Under the terms of the Cedula, grants of land and other inducements were offered to new colonists. To each person of either sex ten quares were allotted, plus half that quantity for each negro slave that any such person should import with him. Any free negro or mulatto coming in to settle "in the quality of an inhabitant and chief of a family" received only half the area of land which would have been granted to him if he were white. The publication of the Cedula resulted in a large influx of French nationals, both white and coloured, with their slaves, from the neighbouring French colonies, and the influx was further increased following the French revolution of 1789, when many of the aristocratic French families who fled France joined their compatriots in Trinidad.

Sir Hugh Wooding, in a lecture given at the Port of Spain Library in 1959, used these facts to explain 'the existence of what I may call a French land-owning aristocracy in an island which at no time belonged to France — an aristocracy which remained a dominant minority exercising an influence far beyond its wealth and numerical strength, and which continued to exercise that influence for nearly a century and a half until it became submerged suddenly sugar and remorselessly, beneath the on-rush of political advancement during the last thirty years." The differentiation between the whites and the coloureds in relation to the size of their land grant was a major factor in the establishment of the social structure which was to emerge. Wooding goes on:

"It will be recalled that when referring to the Cedula issued by the King of Spain on 24th November, 1783, I mentioned that provision was made for the grant of land to any free negro or mulatto coming in to settle in the quality of an inhabitant and chief of a family. It is reasonably certain that there were few, if any, such negroes. But apparently among those admitted and obtaining such grants of land were persons who were described as "free coloured." They stemmed from the miscegenation of some of land owners and certain of their   slave women to whom they were physically attracted. It became a tradition with the French, not only to acknowledge the paternity of their offspring but more to hoist them into a position intermediate between the people of their father's race and those of their mother's." Hence, no doubt, article 12 of the Treaty of Capitulation:-

"The free coloured people who have been acknowledged as such by the laws of Spain shall be protected in their liberty, persons and property, like other inhabitants, they taking the oath of allegiance and

*demeaning themselves as becomes good and peaceful
subjects of His Britannic Majesty."*

"Ranking beneath the "free coloured" were the
comparatively large   number of West African negroes
who, or the ancestors of whom, had been uprooted from
their homes and transported into slavery to cultivate the
fertile fields which had proved such an allurement to M.
Saint-Laurent and his compatriots. Accordingly, when the
British took over, there was a three-tiered community,
comprising the land owning "seigneurs" primarily French
in origin and culture, the free coloured whose pride in their
fathers so transcend any thought of their mothers that
they might well have been born in the "land of the
rooster's egg", and the negro slaves from West Africa
numerically strong but economically impotent. The
significant character of this community was that it was
divided pigmentally as well as economically; the less the
pigmentation, the more they dominated the scene —
governmentally, economically, educationally, socially,
and, indeed, in every other way."

The early French settlers were lucky in that on their
arrival they found that for the first time in its long history of
Spanish ownership, Trinidad had a progressive Governor in Don
Mario Chacon. He welcomed the peaceful invasion from France
and her colonies and gave them every assistance. In return the
industry of the French produced an agrarian revolution as they
established their sugar and cocoa plantations around Port of
Spain and in the fertile valleys of the northern range. Trade and
Commerce increased. The population of the island jumped from
1,400 in 1777 to 10,000 in 1787 and had reached 16,600 when
Chacon capitulated to Abercrombie just ten years later. But
although the British had conquered the island, the French
remained the dominant factor in the community and by one of
those curious tricks of history, Abercrombie brought with him
another Frenchman whose descendants were to further

consolidate the French element and play a not inconsiderable part in the land of their adoption.

Michel Julien de Verteuil was born in France in 1773 and traced his ancestry back to the Lords de Verteuil of the 14th century. He joined the French navy and after an adventurous career, he arrived in England to be granted a commission in the Royal Navy just in time to accompany Abercrombie into Port of Spain. Here, by chance, he met an uncle, the Baron de Gourville, a member of the French colony, who persuaded him to resign his commission and settle in Trinidad. Thus was established one of the largest, and perhaps one of the most influential, families of the French community. One of his sons, Dr. L.A.A. de Verteuil, was a man of many parts and figured prominently in the history of his times as Mayor of Port of Spain and as a member of the Legislative Council until his death in 1900 at the ripe old age of ninety-five. His comprehensive book Trinidad, its Geography, Natural Resources and Prospects, published in 1856 and brought up to date in its second edition in 1884, is an outstanding classic, illustrating as it does, his deep love of country and his extraordinary perception of the problems facing the young colony. This is particularly exemplified in the dedication of his book: "*To the Natives of Trinidad*":

"In dedicating this production to you, my countrymen, I can truly say with Montaigne — '*C'est ici un livre de bonne foy, lecteur.*" I am, therefore, anxious that you should find it truthful, if not as interesting and valuable as it might, under other auspices, have been. And yet, it cannot be reasonably expected that, in treating so many and such varied subjects, no errors should have crept in; this much, however, I can say— they are not wilful errors.

"With all the drawbacks, however, for which I crave your indulgence— I am confident you will find in the work itself material evidences of the great importance of Trinidad in an agricultural as well as an economical point of view. Numberless, varied and more than competent are its resources, but they remain undeveloped still; and it assuredly, in great measure, depends on you to render them available, by cheerfully and unhesitatingly throwing off the lethargy of inaction, by resolutely girding yourselves for the arduous enterprise, and by putting forth, in unity of faith and purpose, the collected might, the energy, the perseverance, of a people resolved to yield to no obstacles, and to halt at no issue short of complete and triumphant success.

"That many obstacles naturally exist, that not a few have been cast in the way, I have admitted and shown; I have also endeavoured to point out such as can be biased to the influence of former social institutions. Nevertheless, on a careful review of our present social condition, you have no cause for despondency; but let my earnest advice prevail with you to sever all connection with the past by a steady advance in moral and industrial improvement; or if the events of the past cannot but be reverted to, if its trials and struggles, its sufferings and humiliation will, of necessity, intrude, let them rather serve as beacons by which to avoid the shocks, and to steer onward and in the current of the future, than as provocations to disunion and precedents for error.

"In conclusion, my opinion on many topics I give up to discussion but I ask and expect a fair and impartial discussion.

Your friend and devoted servant".

The French "Founding Fathers" brought with them the language, culture and religion of their native land and, as they went inland and along the coasts to carve out their estates from the jungle, they never forgot their aristocratic background and the fact that they were here to re-establish their lost fortunes. They considered themselves the social elite and the natural ruling class. As they established themselves on their estates they built their country houses surrounded by pastures for the grazing of their stock and planted their samaan trees for shade.

The estate, as had the ancestral chateau in France, became the centre of economic and social life of the district. The slave, and later the free labourers, looked to the "seigneur" in the big house they as had his lord and master and generally as his friend. Under Chacon they had been the established ruling class. With the capitulation to the British, however, things began to change. A new element was being introduced into the community in the form of British officials and middle class British merchants. The British naturally sought the anglicisation of their new colony but the Frenchmen clung tenaciously to their traditions and their social position.

In spite of the anglicising process in the laws, religion, education and language of the colony, the French element, bound closely by their common heritage and intensely jealous of their position as the "Founding Fathers", retained their identity and remained an exclusive social entity which might well be described, with apologies to J.C. Bossidy's toast to Bostonian Society, as

> "And this was good old Trinidad
> The land of the red cocoa pod
> "Where Ganteaumes spoke only to de Verteuils
> "And de Verteuils spoke only to God. "

Like all the other elements which have gone into the makeup of the multiracial society of Trinidad, the French no doubt had their faults and their shortcomings. And though they clung to their social exclusiveness, and resented the anglicising process of the British, their behaviour was understandable in the circumstances. Dr. de Verteuil expressed their point of view:

> "No matter from whence their ancestors came (and many of them can point to most respectable connections in the old world), the descendants of the first settlers in Trinidad cannot forget that their fathers were the pioneers of civilisation in the islands, that the dense wild forest was first cleared by their energy and perseverance and that there was a time when they had their full influence in the affairs of the colony. They form even now the great majority of the resident proprietory body and, as such, have every right to be treated with consideration instead of being looked down upon by those who are at least but transients."

The French had indeed pioneered civilisation in the island even if one of the attributes of that civilisation was slavery; but there were other attributes which were more lasting and beneficial — the French language and culture, a deep religious sense and an indomitable, pioneering spirit. These were the factors which were to shape the destiny of the island for many decades. They may, as Wooding said, have exercised an influence far beyond their wealth and numerical strength, but it would be difficult to conceive what the history of Trinidad would have been if it weren't for these founding fathers.

CHAPTER II

THE SOCIAL STRUCTURE

WOODING would not have been shocked by his discovery of the three-tiered community on the island at the time of its annexation by the British and the significant character of this community — that it was divided pigmentally as well as economically. That Trinidad should have had a three-tiered community, and still has, is not strange. The three-tiered community has been an established fact in all societies throughout history and will continue to exist as long as the "territorial imperative" — to quote Robert Ardrey — of the animal kingdom (of which man is a part) lasts.

Anthony Wood in his *Nineteenth Century Britain* describes the British Upper Class in this way: "At the top of the social pyramid the aristocracy and wealthy landed families continued to enjoy that pleasant round of elegance and entertainment which had been the unquestioned privilege of the class throughout the eighteenth century. Their world was one of good talk, good food and an easy intimacy with the great men of the day. Land and birth were the main qualifications of those within the charmed circle." The fact is, the three-tiered structure of society was accepted by all England, and was the basis of society in England throughout the 19th century. How could it be different then in the British colonies?

It is true, of course, that in Trinidad, the society was divided "pigmentally as well as economically", or, to put it very bluntly that it was divided on a colour basis. But the division can be better understood if we examine the antecedents of the various races which went to make up the community.

Saint-Laurent's white colonists were of the privileged class before they arrived on the scene. The majority were of aristocratic background. They were well educated and relatively wealthy and the larger land grants handed out to them under the terms of the Cedula entrenched their position further. Chacon accepted them as part of the ruling class and consulted them on matters of public interest. In the state of the colony as it was, they fell naturally into the position of the Upper Class. The free coloured colonists on the other hand were not as well off either educationally or economically and, in turn, received smaller land grants, so it was only natural that they should have fallen in a mid position between the white ruling class and the African slaves. Their origin was rooted in both classes. The Africans, on the other hand, by reason of their slave status constituted the labouring class, and like their counterpart, the labouring class in England, had few privileges, no education and little chance of advancement. Added to this was the fact that climatic conditions precluded the whites from field labour. The European working class who emigrated over this period sought the more temperate climates of America and Canada. There was little, if any, infusion of white labour into the tropics and so the African and later the East Indian became synonymous with the labouring class.

The pattern of class distinction in the West Indies evolved, therefore, out of the hereditary background of its constituent parts and was little different to that of 19th century Britain where social and economic standing were firmly rooted in the family tree. Throughout the 19th century the British clung to the cliché that the battle of Waterloo had been won on the playing fields of Eton — which was a neat way of expressing their credo that only the aristocracy could lead or govern. Appointments in the army, the civil service, and even the church were reserved for the gentry.

This is clearly illustrated by a letter among my family papers. Great grandfather Dr. O'Connor had submitted an application through his friend Major-General Sir John Webb seeking the admission of his eldest son as a cadet to the Royal Academy of Woolwich. Sir John in his reply datelined Woolwich 1841 showed some surprise that his friend should entertain any hope that his application would be successful:

"For whereas the number of such applications is so great and the great majority backed by political interests that in almost every case the person to be selected is a question of influence and the candidate whose friends have the strongest claims on the Master General has naturally the best prospects of being preferred"

And he went on to explain that, after all, Dr. O'Connor had merely been a Lieutenant Surgeon during his army career!

It was only through the slow process of education as it was extended to the lower orders in England during the mid-nineteenth century that a few of the labouring class began to emerge from their traditional environment and rise in the social and economic scale.

With the introduction of free education and scholarships to the universities, it now became possible for the youth of the labouring class to enter the professional ranks and as he rose in his profession so he rose in the social and economic structure and, as an eminent surgeon or Q.C., he became accepted at the house parties of the landed gentry and was admitted to the exclusive clubs. In a changing society the privileges of birth gave way to those of education and achievement. The pattern has been the same in the West Indies where the spread of education had opened the doors for the members of the traditional working class to reach the highest peaks of the social and economic structure.

In spite of the tremendous educational attainments of the coloured races and their economic advancements in all fields, their social acceptance by the old guard social elite was a slow process. To understand this, if not to excuse it, one must remember the origin of this social elite who set, no doubt, the pattern of the white community over the years. André Maurois quotes Tocqueville as writing in the 18th century:

"If you seek another application of the science of language to that of history, trace through time and space the destiny of the word gentleman, which sprang from the French "gentilhomme." You will see its meaning spreading in England in proportion as social class approximate. With successive centuries it is used of men of standing in the social scale. But in France the word gentilhomme always remained strictly confined to its original meaning. The word was preserved intact as serving to indicate the members of a caste, because the caste itself had been preserved, as much separated from all others as it ever was."

It was this caste concept which kept the French families as a thing apart in the social environment of the island and enabled them to exercise the influence which they did in the social customs and manners of the colony. They had established their social territory and like every other territorial animal, they resented any intrusion from outside. In this they were no different from the English or Irish landed gentry, who were just as hesitant to accept the middle and lower classes into their family or social circle. I recall my schooldays in Ireland. There I spent my holidays with a "County" family. Their farming interests were transacted through the small-town solicitor and bank manager but neither was ever invited to dinner! The caste line was ever present.

Donald Wood in Trinidad in Transition: The Years After Slavery deals at length with the colour barriers of the post emancipation era. In his chapter "*The Creoles and Society*" he states: "There were enough letters in the Press during the period to make it certain that the general nuance of manner riled the sensitive as much as particular instances of discrimination. Collegatarius in 1858, for example, asserted that white men only treated educated coloureds as familiar equals during business discussions but that outside "the mart" relations dried up." Not very different to my Irish friends!

Whatever the shortcomings and prejudices of French Creole society, it lived by the inherited tenets of "*Noblesse oblige*" and being "*comme il faut*". The family was the unit, and pride of family was uppermost in their minds. The women folk were ladies, gentle and unsophisticated, engaged in the supervision of their homes, doing fine needlework, and, in Port of Spain, taking the air in their carriages around the Pitch Walk in the cool of the afternoon. It was a society by no means rich but sufficiently well off to educate its sons in the best English public schools and its daughters at exclusive French convents.

From these seats of learning, the more brilliant sons returned with a profession in medicine or law to serve their country while the less ambitious joined the Civil Service and were good and honest servants as Wardens or Magistrates, or took over the management of their fathers' estates. The young ladies, on the other hand, returned from their convents to take their place in society, and, chaperoned by their parents to the occasional private ball or to a reception at Government House, awaited a good match. They lived in a world apart, a gracious gentle life, although the estate house, far out in the country, to which many a young bride moved, was a far cry from luxurious living.

Charles Kingsley, strolling down Frederick Street in 1870, described the scene:

> "Here come from the convent school two coloured young ladies, probably pretty, possibly lovely, certainly gentle, modest and well-dressed according to the fashions of Paris or New York, and here comes the unmistakable Englishman, tall, fair, close-shaven, arm in arm with another man whose delicate features, more sallow complexion and little moustache mark him as some Frenchman or Spaniard of old family. Both are dressed as if they were going to walk up Pall-Mall or the Rue de Rivoli; for "go-to-meeting clothes" are somewhat too much de rigueur here; a shooting jacket and wideawake betrays the newly-landed Englishman. Both take off their hats with a grand air to a lady in a carriage, for they are very fine gentlemen, and well that is for the civilisation of the island, for it is from such men that the good manners for which the West Indies are or ought to be famous, have permeated down"

Kingsley's description of the impeccably dressed gentleman doffing his hat, with a grand air, to his lady friend might well have been written forty years later to describe my father as 1 walked up Frederick Street with him. The social pattern had changed very little by 1910. What a pity it is that in building our new structure we would demolish the pleasing façade of the old!

CHAPTER III

ENTER THE O'CONNORS

MY great grandfather, James Lynch O'Connor, was a surgeon in the British Army. He served in the Napoleonic wars and was present at the battle of Waterloo, attached to a Company of the Royal Artillery. When his Company was posted to Trinidad in 1817, he accompanied it. What, I wonder, were the feelings of this young surgeon at his first sight of Trinidad?

After weeks at sea on a crowded troop ship, his spirits must have lifted at the beauty of the scene as he entered the Boca, only to be dashed at the depressing shore line of Port of Spain. The area south of Marine Square, now Independence Square, was swampland with a few huts. Yet, it was a busy quay and there were signs of progress: Dozens of mule carts were transporting fill from the Laventille hills in an effort to reclaim the swamp area between the south side of Marine Square and what is today South Quay.

We can picture the young surgeon falling-in on the quayside with his company, and as slaves load the soldiers' sea chests onto carts, he and his fellow officers are introduced to the senior officers of the garrison who had ridden down from Fort George. Then, the march up Frederick Street in the mud and slush, with the dirty drains full of refuse running down the centre of the street. And while the cows, dogs and pigs rummaging in the garbage scurry off before the advancing troop, the town population rushes to see what the new arrivals look like and to wave their greetings.

The troop may have been cheered up a bit as they marched past Woodford Square and saw more signs of progress. A low wall was being built to enclose it and to keep out the cows and pigs, and trees were being planted to improve its appearance. As they reached Park Street they would have turned left and marched out into the country along the route of Tragarete Road, a dirt track leading out into the sugar-cane lands of Ariapita and Woodbrook, and then the steep climb up to their quarters at Fort George.

What was Port of Spain like in 1817? From the small fishing village which had greeted the arrival of Saint-Laurent's Frenchmen, it had sprung to life and was now a growing and prosperous town reaching out westwards beyond Frederick Street as well as northwards. The sea still washed against the foundations of the wooden Roman Catholic Church on Tamarind Square and continued to do so long after the Cathedral had been completed in 1832. However, though the town was growing in size, its amenities were not keeping pace with its growth in spite of Governor Woodford's herculean efforts. The streets were unpaved and uncleaned. Sanitation consisted of cesspits in the backyards side-by-side with the water well which was the only water supply available to the householder. It was not until 1829 that water was brought into the city by an aqueduct from the St. Ann's River. There were no schools, no hospital and few doctors.

In 1823, the National School for Boys was established by the Cabildo and this was followed by one for girls three years later. A Mr. Evans was the first master of the boys' school; he was brought in from England. Could this have been the D. Evans later Chaplain to the Forces, who in July 1841 wrote this glowing recommendation for my grandfather?

"I certify that the bearer Philip Charles O'Connor who is about 16 years old was under my tuition in 1830 until he went home in 1836 and about ten months since his return last year. He is possessed of superior abilities in acquisition of languages; can speak French fluently, writes it grammatically, understands Latin and Greek so as to be able to construe Caesar's Commentaries, Virgil and the Greek Testament with facility, can work all the problems in the first book of Euclid and has lately commenced to learn Algebra and the German Language in both of which he has made great progress considering the short time he has been studying them. He is of a docile and amicable disposition and I can say of him what can be said of but a few that I have never known him to utter a falsehood, of which he has the greatest abhorrence, he is in fact what every parent would like his child to be, free from vice and guile and may he always continue to be so.'

With the shortage of doctors and the growing population, it was not surprising that Dr. O'Connor should on his arrival have applied to Sir Ralph Woodford and obtained a "License to Practise Physic and Surgery in the Island." This permitted him to go into private practice, which he did with some degree of success, as his marriage contract with Miss Sophie le Fer in 1822 testifies. This formidable document of sixteen pages in imposing script was drawn up between the parties by Mr. Raymond Garcia (Advocate) and dated September 1822. He endowed his future wife with, among other assets,

"The rights and interests and share in the outstanding debts due the partnership concern established between him and Doctor Alexander Williams, M.D. amounting to 2,302 pounds 17 shillings and one penny. As well as Lot No.11 together with the Dwelling House and Buildings and Premises thereon situated in Abercrombie Street."

Today there is a sign at the corner of Abercrombie Street and Independence Square South which reads:

ABERCROMBIE STREET
ANNO DOMINI 1822

The doctor's house must therefore have been one of the earliest on the newly opened street. In 1823, he was appointed "staff surgeon to the Military Forces vice Neilson promoted". General Sir John Webb, Director of the Ordnance Department Woolwich, appears to have taken a keen interest in the career of the young surgeon and corresponded regularly with him. Their correspondence over the years throws some interesting light on conditions at the time. In 1825, two years after his marriage, Sir John wrote him:

"As you have been some years established at Trinidad, and are as I am informed, become a family man, I presume your present views and pursuits in life are incompatible with the obligations you are under of returning to the Department and recommencing duty as a Second Assistant Surgeon at the bottom of the list. Unger this impression I am desirous to inform you that if you wish to solicit the Master General of Ordnance to permit you to transfer to the Retired List on the Half Pay you now receive (for none other can be granted) this is a favourable time for making the attempt. I advise you to take this question into serious consideration and to decide upon it without delay for the period of your being brought on the Effective Establishment, though still uncertain, cannot be far distant and if you await its arrival the power of choosing will be entirely at an end.

"I shall the customary Form for Memorial to the Duke of Wellington to be sketched on the 3rd page of this letter for your guidance in the event of your determining to request to retire. You will be pleased to send me an early answer in duplicate and by two separate and should you resolve to come on full pay, it will be necessary for you to accompany it with a Declaration which any Medical Officer is now required to make that you are rea o take without the least reserve, the most distant or most active service the duties of the Department may require' "

Dr. O'Connor decided to accept Sir John's advice and to retire from the army, but he apparently tried to get something more than his half-pay, as Sir John writes him a private letter on 6th July, 1825.

"I cannot send you the Official Notification of your being permitted to retire from the Department without acknowledging your private letter of 1st May and of assuring you that if the Duke of Wellington had given in any one instance an increase of half-pay I would have made every exertion in my power to have obtained for you the same advantage. But in no case had he ever departed from the strict Regulations of The Service, wherefore it is useless to reiterate requests which are invariably answered with positive refusals.

"If there were any necessity for appointing Ordnance Surgeon at Trinidad I should feel highly gratified in giving you the refusal of it but all such appointments in the West Indies have been abolished for reasons it is unnecessary to state but which will prevent their ever being restored for it has been determined by the Master General and Board, to meet all such wants by Military means.

"As our official connection is now terminated, I close our correspondence with requesting you to believe that I have always highly esteemed your character and approved of your conduct and that I shall at all times be rejoiced to hear of your prosperity and happiness."

In spite of his not having got an increase in his half-pay, the post of Ordnance Surgeon, Dr. O'Connor's services nevertheless were made use of frequently by the Government and by the Military Forces in the island. It is recorded in Brigade Orders of 22nd May, 1834, No. 2:

"Dr. Doyle, Principal Medical Officer, Dr. Savery 1st West Indian Regiment, Surgeon Waterson 19th

Regiment and Staff Assistant Wood, having under order from the Deputy Adjutant General gone to Barbados.

'The following arrangements in the Medical Department of the Island shall take place until the receipt of instructions from Headquarters.

"J.L.O'Connors Esq. M.D. will take charge of the Hospital at St. Jame Barracks receiving one pound sterling per diem from Monday the 19th inst. inclusive.

'TV. Meikleh Esq. M.D. will take Medical charge of the Post at San Fernando at the rate of 7/6 per diem from Saturday the 17th inst.

"Asist. Surgeon G.K. Smith, 67 Regiment will take charge of the 1st West Indian Regiment and will also take upon himself the duties of Principal Medical Officer in Trinidad."

In September 1837, a letter datelined Government House addressed to Dr. Dr. O'Connor reads:

"His Excellency Sir G. Hill begs to acquaint Dr. O'Connor that the Council of Government at its meeting yesterday noted that the sum of sixty pounds sterling should be paid to Dr. O'Connor as a remuneration for his services In attending upon and vaccinating the poor in Barrio No. 3. during the existence of smallpox in this town.

"His Excellency takes this opportunity of expressing to doctor O'Connor his acknowledgments for the ready manner in which he undertook to perform this important duty and for the services he rendered in performance of the same".

While in March 1839 Dr. Loinsworth, Surgeon to the Forces, wrote him:

" I cannot quit the colony without expressing to you the high sense I feel for the professional assistance you have at all times afforded this Garrison but particularly during the late epidemic that occurred at St. James barracks in which officers on men suffered so severely."

Doctor O'Connor was evidently a man of high moral standing and humanitarian views as his report on the conditions of the slaves in certain estate hospitals which he visited in the Chaguanas area in July 1827 shows. The preamble to this report throws interesting light on the mode of travel in Trinidad in his day.

"On Saturday 21st July I proceeded from town to the quarter Chaguanas. I was, according to appointment, at the Kung's Wharf at 10:00 o'clock AM but inconsequence of some repairs the boat required it was detained to 11:00 o'clock. Having a headwind with frequent squalls and rain I did not arrive at Chaguanas until 2:00 PM when I immediately proceeded to Felicite Estate. As there were no sick in the hospital Mr. McChesney furnished me with a mule and I proceeded without a moment's delay to the Edinburgh estate".

His report takes the estate management seriously to task for the conditions existing in its hospital. There were evidently suggestions by the management that he was being too partial to the slaves for he writes:

"I am perfectly indifferent to the opinion of any man in the performance of so sacred a duty as that of umpire between the respective duties of Master and slave for during the nine years I have practised amongst slaves, I have invariably used every exertion to prevent the slaves imposing on their masters (and to which that class are with few exceptions inevitably prone) and at the same time whenever a slave was ill treated I have procured him justice."

In his report, he accuses the managers of the estate of "being determined to get rid of Medical attendance as they fancy it will interfere with their prerogatives and probably afford you (the owner) too much information respecting the unheard of mortality that prevailed on all your properties during the last 12 months." He referred to "the different estates I now attend or have attended during the past eight years", which suggests that he had a considerable practice as a visiting doctor to various estates but, unfortunately, he gives no Indication as to where these estates were situated and how far afield he travelled as a result of his estate practice. Presumably, they were the estates around Port of Spain as the areas of Laventille, Woodbrook, St. Clair, St. Ann's, Belmont, Maraval, Diego Martin and Chaguanas were all under sugar cultivation.

Dr. O'Connor died a comparatively young man in Barbados in 1845 where he had gone due to failing health. The high esteem in which he was held by all who knew him is confirmed by Father Roger's letter datelined the R.C. Presbytery, Bridgetown, December 1845, to Father Lee in Port of Spain:

"I am truly grieved to say that it becomes my melancholy duty to announce to you afflicting intelligence of the death of our most excellent and respected friend Dr. James Lynch O'Connor whose sickness and danger I mentioned in my last letter. I cannot bring myself to write directly to his widowed lady but I beg you to break the sad news to her. His funeral was most respectable, numbers of Protestant gentlemen of the highest rank and of every profession as well as Catholics attending with their carriages both the chapel (nearly half a mile) and the Cemetery."

In his comparatively short career of 28 years in Trinidad, Dr. O'Connor fathered a family of six sons and one daughter. As there were no schools in the island, his sons were all educated in his native Ireland and returned to play a not inconsiderable part in the history of their generation. Three of them, one my grandfather, founded the firm of "O'Connor Bros." with offices on South Quay and were the first agents for the Compagnie Générale Transatlantique. One was a Magistrate and one was Crown Solicitor and the Mayor of Port of Spain from 1864 — 1865, while an O'Connor is mentioned among the "large number of Roman Catholic Gentry" present at the inauguration of Queen's Royal College by the Governor in 1870.

During his short career in Trinidad, Dr. O'Connor witnessed many far-reaching changes in the life of the Colony. The most important of these was the abolition of slavery in August 1834 and the tremendous impact which this was to have on the entire community both economically and socially. The impact of Emancipation and the thinking of some of his contemporaries is brought out in his correspondence with Sir John Webb. Datelined Woolwich 1st August 1837 Sir John wrote:

"I have had the pleasure to receive your obliging letter of March last and also some Colonial Newspapers the perusal of which shows very plainly that I am become a great stranger to Trinidad (yourself excepted) as if I never been in the island. While my local interest is thus worn out, I am glad to learn that the agricultural interests of the planters are somewhat more encouraging. It is their lot in common with tie landholders throughout the West Indies to have to endure the consequences of a very momentous and extensive change. No man of any principle can advocate the cause of slavery and yet the chief weight of abolishing this enormous evil falls on the present generation with an almost overwhelming degree of pressure. Amongst the many embarrassments that result from it the most perplexing is that of the negro being totally ignorant of the nature of relative duties; wherefore their expectations are unguided by any of those principles which influence the conduct of civilised people and tend so importantly to promote the peace and happiness of society. The step, however, has been taken and instruction is the only remedy. It will undoubtedly be a slow one but with patience and perseverance, aided by experience of the obligations and necessities that arise out of the general exchange in the relations of life will ultimately lead, as I earnestly hope, to settled peace and prosperity in each of the islands."

Apart from Emancipation other changes had taken place. Port of Spain had taken on the shape of things to come. The town been extended northwards by the purchase of the St. Ann's estate from the Peschier family. The Queen's Park Savannah had been laid out for the grazing of cattle and for recreation, and the first racing meeting had been held in 1828. The Pitch Walk circled the Savannah and the residential area was moving out around it. The Botanical Gardens had been established and a new Governor's residence erected in what is today Government House Grounds. The Colonial Hospital and St. James Barracks had been erected. The swamp and dumping ground which lay between King Street (now Independence Square North) and South Quay had been reclaimed. Independence Square had been laid out with walls and gardens where the military band played on Sunday afternoons.

Life in general had become more pleasant and bearable. The Ice House Company was importing ice and frozen meat which the sold at 25 cents per pound. Pipe borne water was available from the St. Ann's river and plans were afoot for the Maraval reservoir. Facilities had been provided by the Colonial Bank and a fortnightly steamship service between the colony and England had been established the Royal Mail Steam Packet Company.

The countryside, too, had been opened up. Port of Spain was linked to San Fernando and Arima by road. Sugar cultivation had extended along the West coast to as far south as La Brea and even to Cedros which was connected to Port of Spain by a regular ship service.

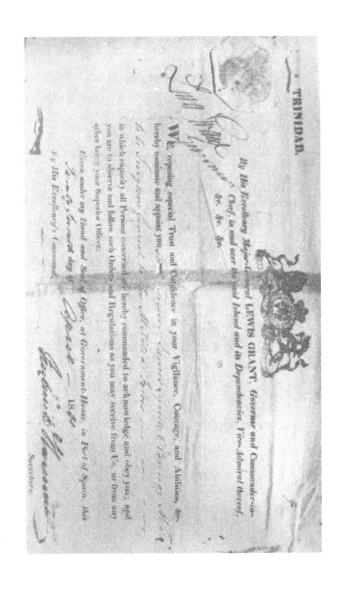

TRINIDAD.

By His Excellency Sir RALPH JAMES WOODFORD, Bart. Governor and Commander in Chief in and over The said Island and its Dependencies, Vice-Admiral of The same, and President of The Illustrious Board of Cabildo, &c. &c. &c.

Ralph James Woodford

ON the Report of the President of the Medical Board, Licence is hereby to Mr. *James Lynch O'Connor* to practise Physic and Surgery, in the said Island, under the Proclamation of the December, 1814, and otherwise according to Law.

Given under my Hand, this *Third* day of *November*

By Command of His Excellency,

COMPAGNIE
Générale Transatlantique

LE PUBLIC est invité à prendre note des importantes modifications que viennent de faire la **COMPAGNIE GENERALE TRANSATLANTIQUE** dans son

SERVICE DES PASSAGERS.

Sur la ligne des Antilles la Compagnie vient d'établir une nouvelle catégorie de passagers de chambre; ces passagers seront reçus sur les paquebots aux prix suivants :

Francs ou 150 *Dollars*

De St. Nazaire à St. Thomas la Martinique,
la Guadeloupe, le Cap-Haïtien, Santiago
de Cuba, la Havane, Puerto-Rico,
la Jamaïque, Santa Martha, Colon,
La Guayra, Puerto-Cabello,
Trinidad et vice-versa.

50 *Francs ou* 175 *Dollars*

De St. Nazaire à la Véra-Cruz, Démerarie,
Surinam, Cayenne et vice-versa.

C'est dans les cabines intérieures du 1er pont et du 2me pont que seront placés ces passagers qui, du reste, seront traités absolument de la même manière que tous les autres passagers de chambre.

La Compagnie désirant aussi aller au devant d'une classe très nombreuse de ...

LES Passagers d'Entrepont

a réduit son tarif pour cette catégorie de voyageurs aux prix suivants :

100 *Francs ou* 80 *Dollars*

De St. Nazaire à St. Thomas, la Martinique,
la Guadeloupe, Porto-Rico, la Havane,
Trinidad et vice-versa.

150 *Francs ou* 90 *Dollars*

De St. Nazaire à Puerto-Cabello, La Guayra,
Santa Martha Colon et vice-versa.

200 *Francs ou* 100 *Dollars*

De St. Nazaire au Cap-Haïtien, Santiago
de Cuba, la Jamaïque, Démerarie, Surinam,
Cayenne, Vera-Cruz et vice-versa.

Le tarif du fret, retour sur St. Nazaire reste le même, où les soussignés sont autorisés à ...

CHAPTER IV

SLAVERY

THE epoch of slavery in Trinidad was relatively short when compared with the rest of the Caribbean and the southern United States. Slavery had been in existence for centuries in the New World and had reached its peak in the 17th and 18th centuries but it did not touch Trinidad until St. Laurent's French settlers came in with their slaves in the 1780s. While the other islands had been busy establishing their sugar and cotton plantations, the Spanish during their 300 years of occupancy had done nothing to develop the agricultural potential of Trinidad and, hence, they saw no need for slave labour. Only five years before the advent of St. Laurent, the population of the island consisted of 340 Europeans, 870 free mulattoes and 200 slaves. Twenty years later, it had grown to 28,000 of whom 20,000 were slaves.

Not only was the epoch of slavery short in Trinidad (it was to last only 50 years), but it was free also from many of the evils and brutalities which characterised it in the other islands and in an earlier epoch. The reason for this was, as Dr. Williams has pointed out in his History of the People of Trinidad and Tobago, that Trinidad was not a plantation society in the days of slavery; it was rather a society of small estates. The average number of slaves per estate was only seven — 80% of the estates had only ten and only 17% had more than a hundred. Another significant point was the large ratio of domestic to field workers, and as the domestic was better treated than the field worker, this was the reason (historians believe) for the more amicable relationship between master and slave in Trinidad than was the case in the other islands.

These were not the only factors which alleviated the lot of the slave in Trinidad. Soon after the arrival of the French settlers Chacon introduced his Code Noir for the protection of the slaves whom he permitted the French to bring in with them. The Code Noir gave considerable protection to the slaves, and was, perhaps the first "Labour Code" in history. Some of its main clauses were:

1.   All owners of slaves were obliged to instruct them in the principles of the Roman Catholic religion and were not to allow them to work on religious holidays. At the end of every day's work, the slaves were to say the Rosary in the presence of their masters.

2.   The Justices of the districts were to determine the quality and quantity of the food given daily to the slaves.

3.   Two hours daily were allowed to the slaves for work on their own account. No slave was to work over the age of 60 or below 17 and the women slaves were to be employed in work appropriate to their sex.

4.   The slave owners were to provide "commodious habitations" for the slaves with beds, blankets and other necessities. Each slave was to have his own bed and there were to be not more than two occupants to a room.

5.   Slaves who, on account of old age or illness, were unable to work, were to be maintained by their masters who were not to give them their liberty in order to get rid of them.

6.   Masters or stewards who failed in the obligations imposed on them by the Code were subject to a fine of $50 for the first offence, $100 for the second and $200 for the third offence.

While Chacon's Code Noir had only nine years to run before the British conquered the island, the British parliament at the date of conquest was already committed to the abolition of the slave trade and the gradual elimination of slavery. Popular feeling in England and elsewhere was running high in favour of the total elimination of the system. It was natural, therefore, that England should be concerned with all the aspects of slavery in its newly acquired colony and from the very outset Britain made it clear that the labour force in Trinidad was not to be supplemented by African slaves. The result of this was the development of a phenomenal slave transfer from some of the less prosperous islands and between 1813 and 1821 Trinidad received over 3,500 slaves from the other islands. This ruse, however, failed to alleviate the acute shortage of labour for the rapidly expanding cocoa and sugar industries and various efforts were made to recruit labour from other sources.

Williams summarises the position thus:

"While all their efforts were being made to recruit labour from all parts of the globe, slave labour was becoming increasingly difficult, at least on the old terms. As Trinidad was a model British slave colony the British Government experimented with it for the introduction of ameliorating measures to satisfy the criticisms of the abolitionists in England. The most important of them was the Order in Council of 1823 which the British Government hoped, after its introduction in Trinidad, would be adopted in the self-governing colonies".

The Order in Council went even further than Chacon's Code Noir and it raised considerable wrath among the planters in Trinidad. But their opposition was not towards improving the rank of the slave, it was against interference by the Government. To quote Gertrude Carmichael in *her History of the West Indian Islands of Trinidad and Tobago:*

"The planters, led by Burnley, were not questioning the Order in Council on the rights or wrongs of amelioration of the conditions of the slaves. They resented the interference of the law knowing that in the whole of the West Indies there was no other colony where slaves were so well treated as in Trinidad. They would not have opposed making obligatory by law what has been the custom of the colony for many years had they not seen in the Order in Council the next step towards complete emancipation and the probable ruin of their estates.

"As an 'institution' there was no argument in favour of slavery. Though legally the slave had no rights, in Trinidad there were many privileges to which he was entitled by tradition and common usage.

"Medical attention, support in old age, Christmas, New Year and Easter gifts, supplies of clothing and many other comforts, were all part and parcel of the master-slave relationship in the colony. There had, of course, been individual cases of cruelty and ill-usage but these the authorities punished severely. Many of the planters thought it unfair that the Order in Council should be tried out in Trinidad, where arrangements were better than in the other colonies and that when the law turned custom into obligation all kindly feelings would disappear."

In spite of the opposition of the planters, the Order in Council was proclaimed in May 1824 and came into force on June 25. The planters were not happy over the outcome. They saw the writing on the wall that emancipation was in the offing. Mrs. Carmichael analyses their point of view:

"Though many did not consider slavery, per se, to be anything but an outrage on humanity, they felt that its existence was not their fault and that it was unfair to ask them to bear the cost of its removal. Slaves represented earned or inherited wealth. This wealth was now to be taken away from them by a political party which was using the cause of humanity to appease the opposition in Parliament. A more cheerful and optimistic view might have been taken in Trinidad if the planter had been assured that the benevolent Government which was taking away his living was as particular to stop all forms of brutality in its own country as in bettering the condition of the slaves in Trinidad"

While no one can possibly condone the slave trade, and man's inhumanity to man which it engendered, Mrs. Carmichael's reference to the conditions of the working class in England at this period suggests that it is in this context (the context of the times) that slavery in Trinidad should be viewed if we are to arrive at a true perspective. Andre Maurois *in A History of England*, writing on conditions after the cessation of the Napoleonic wars, notes:

"It could not be expected that a House of Commons which was a little more than a club of gentlemen farmers, fully occupied with the wars against Napoleon, could have imposed strict and sound regulations on the factories and towns during the years of their growth. But the outcome was a disgrace to a rich and free country — In the mines half naked women were employed as mere beasts of burden, and children spent their days in the darkness of the pit-gallery, opening and shutting air vents. In the lace industry infants of four years were employed —

"A Factory Act of 1819 controlled the employment of children under nine years old who at the beginning of the century had worked as much as fifteen or sixteen hours daily in the cotton mills. An Act of 1833 limited the employment of workers under eighteen and set up the first factory inspectors. In 1847 the hours of work for women were limited to ten.

"At the time of the Reform Act (1832) the condition of the poor in town and country was appalling. Disraeli and Dickens depicted these Two Nations in their novels — 'The Nation of the Rich" and "The Nation of the Poor" living side by side each cut off from the other. The rural labourers' cottage was often a mere hovel around which ran children in rags and tatters. These villagers just contrived to keep body and soul together by eking out their wretched pittance with poaching and alms".

The conditions in the towns were no better, perhaps even worse:

"Where thousands of families lived in squalor and dirt with the drinking water polluted by odours, the pestilential courtyards where even grass would not grow, the cellars flooded with stagnant water where ten to twelve people slept.

"In the town of Bath the normal life span of a gentleman was 55 years, that of a worker 25".

Maurois' reference to 'The Two Nations" — the nation of the rich and the nation of the poor — is taken from Disraeli's novel *Sybil or, the Two Nations* in which the following passage occurs:

"'Well, society may be in its infancy," said Egremont, slightly smiling: "but, say what you like, our Queen reigns over the greatest nation that ever existed."

"Which nation?" asked the stranger, "for she reigns over two."

The stranger paused; Egremont was silent, but looked enquiringly. "Yes", resumed the younger stranger after a moment's interval. "Two nations; between whom there is no intercourse and no sympathy; who are as ignorant of each other's habits, thoughts and feelings, as if they were dwellers in different zones, or inhabitants of different planets; who are formed by different breeding, are fed by different food, are ordered by different manners and are not governed by the same laws".

"You speak of – "said Egremont hesitatingly, 'THE RICH and THE POOR".

As late as 1848 — 1849 cholera raged in England and Anthony Wood in his *Nineteenth Century Britain* records:

"The ravages of the second summer were particularly frightful. I yesterday was with W. and M. over the cholera districts of Bermondsey", wrote Charles Kingsley to his wife, "and oh, God, what I saw, people having no water to drink — hundreds of them — but the water in the common sewer which stagnated full of dead fish and dogs under their windows." Is it any wonder that Kingsley found the "natives" and the East Indian immigrants happy when he visited Trinidad a few years after his experiences in London? The poor in Trinidad may have been slaves but the poor in England were not free. The labouring class in England in the early eighteenth century had few rights, they had little education and no vote. England, too, had its "traditionally dispossessed" in the slums of Manchester and Liverpool and they, too, were seeking emancipation. The voice of labour was being heard and feared. Maurois tells us —

"Fear is always cruel: rebellious workmen and rustics were sent to the gallows or to Botany Bay. The Horse Guards went out into the country districts and more than once blood flowed. The most serious massacre was near Manchester in 1819 when the troops fired on the crowd leaving eleven dead and numerous wounded".

These are bits of English history we do not learn in school, but which when read in the context of Chacón's Code Noir and the Order in Council of 1824 place the evils of slavery in a truer perspective, and should cause us to wonder: Was the slave in Trinidad better or worse off than his counterpart, the British labouring class? Picton, Trinidad's first English Governor, had answered the question. In one of his despatches he wrote:

"I came to this country nine years ago with a strong impression against the system (slavery). Few, I believe, can pretend to have more experience or better opportunities of examining the state of slavery in these islands than I can and I shall not hesitate to say that the slaves of this island, generally taken, are in point of comfort and care at least equal to a great majority of

European peasantry…a few masters, blind to their own interests, probably do treat their slaves with less humanity. The law should in such cases take cognisance of such conduct and punish it as they do here".

The epoch of slavery was a degrading chapter in the history of mankind but it is not the only "Black Pages" which shock us today, for it coincided with an era in which man's inhumanity to man was by no means confined to Africa and the West Indies. It coincided with the era when the might of Britain's sea-power rested on the press gangs, the era during which Cromwell, in the name of God, persecuted and killed thousands of Irishmen, the era in which Jeffreys presided over his "Bloody Assize," ordering over 300 executions for high treason. And, it embraced, as we have seen, the Industrial Revolution with the appalling conditions under which the English working class barely survived.

CHAPTER V

THE EAST INDIANS

THE system of indentured labour under which the East Indian immigrants were introduced to Trinidad has been severely criticised. It has been termed harsh and inhuman and likened to a modified form of slavery. As in the case of slavery, however, it should be viewed in the context of the times. The mid-nineteenth century, as has been seen, was a harsh period for the poor and the labouring classes in England; it was even harsher in other countries of the old world and the poor and the dispossessed were moving out to seek a new life in the New World. The Irish and the Poles were crowding into insanitary sailing ships to sweat and toil with pick and shovel on the laying of the railway lines across the United States; the Chinese were doing the same and died in their thousands from rock-falls, avalanches and the early experiments with explosives as they blasted the railways through the Rockies into California. In the West Indies it was the same: violent death from disease, cruelty and natural disaster was the fate of thousands of plantation workers.

The East Indians who came to Trinidad did so in search of a new life and if we examine our development from a slave and indentured society to a free society, it is dishonest to maintain that the majority did not find it for themselves and their children. They came to escape from the squalor of the Indian towns, the periodic floods and droughts with their attendant famine, and the Caste System which had kept them in bondage for centuries. It may be argued that they jumped from the frying-pan into the fire, but the fire of indenture was to last only five years while in India the frying pan still sizzles with famine and poverty.

The barrack-room system on the estates left much to be desired but was it better or worse than the slums of Madras and Calcutta? The death rate among the early immigrants was high but was it higher than amongst the poor in India? These questions are not to exonerate a system that was evil and humiliating, but to put our history in the right perspective.

The first East Indians arrived in Trinidad in 1845 and numbered 219; during the next year a further 1,556 were admitted. Owing to various problems, however, the influx was suspended during 1849 and 1851 but the flow was started again in 1852. To quote Gertrude Carmichael:

"When immigration reopened in 1852, the type of immigrant improved. A new order in council introduced several safeguards, including the presence of a Protector of Immigrants in the Legislative Councils of the Colonies concerned. Terms of indenture were strictly laid down, ample provision was made for food, lodging, wages, medical attention and return passages.

"The return of so many immigrants affected the finances of the colony. Later in 1865 when repatriation reached its peak, the British Trident sailed for India with over 12,000 pounds in cash on board. To counteract this alarming loss of sterling, Crown lands were offered to immigrants and a large East Indian community gradually came into being, supplemented by those who, finding conditions better in Trinidad, returned from India. From 1851 to 1917 there was a continuous stream of East Indians entering Trinidad and Demerara."

The decision to offer Crown lands to the East Indians in lieu of their return passages was a major milestone in the history of the island and when this was followed by the Ordinance of 1886 reducing the price of Crown lands to 1 pound per acre, thus placing land within the reach of the poor man, the East Indian found his place in our society. Williams records that "between 1885 and 1895 a total of 22,916 acres was sold to Indian immigrants between 1902 and 1912, 4,450 grants totalling 31,766 acres were distributed, the Indians paying 72,837 pounds for them."

Thus was built up that society of small land owners and cane farmers which Dr. de Verteuil had so wisely advocated when he wrote:

"The establishment of central factories will encourage the formation of a middle-class, by affording to small proprietors the means of manufacturing into sugar whatever quantity of canes they may plant. I have always been convinced that the existence of such a body is a necessary element in the welfare of all communities, but particularly of those which are chiefly or solely addicted to agricultural pursuits. Wherever such a class does not exist, there is an immense gap left open, which the lower classes will invariably attempt to fill up, either by forcing themselves through or dragging the higher classes into the same, thus creating permanent danger to the social institutions. This danger is greatly mitigated, if not entirely obviated, when there is a graduation established from the lowest up to the highest. Those who start from below and above to meet midway must interchange ideas in their progress upwards and downwards, and form as an intermediate link between the two extremities of the social scale. The formation of a class of industrious small proprietors was therefore desirable, and ought to have been encouraged, not by granting privileges, as I have heard it contended, but by removing, instead of throwing obstacles in the way."

The lot of the indentured labourer was not as hard, in all cases, as has been depicted in some quarters. I can recall the first group allocated to our estate in 1908. New barracks had been erected for them, as required by the Ordinance. The group consisted of ten men and two women. They arrived with few possessions, the clothes in which they stood and a few pots and pans, but they were cheerful and happy. They spoke no English but we children conversed with them through an interpreter, and I can remember the excitement and joy of the group on their first pay day. They had only earned 25 cents per day (the statutory rate) but on their return from the village after their first shopping spree they were anxious and proud to show us their purchases — new shirts for the men and bright cotton prints for the women.

We children quickly learnt to beat their drums and helped to build the tadjahs for the Hosein festival, while they quickly learnt the estate work and became good and efficient labourers. At the end of their five-year indenture most of them remained with us.

One of the sons of this group, born on the estate, is today a prosperous taxi-owner, free and independent. What, one wonders, would have been his future had he been born in India? He is just one of the many who found a better life in Trinidad. Thousands have done far better, as successful businessmen, as agriculturalists, and in the professions. Do any of these, one wonders, lament the fact that their forefathers braved the hardships of indenture in search of a better life?

CHAPTER VI

THE YEARS AFTER EMANCIPATION

"BEHIND its beautiful facade, Trinidad in the decades after emancipation was a harsh, wild land. Men had scarcely begun to tame it". (Donald Wood: *Trinidad in Transition: The Years after Slavery*).

The map of Trinidad dated 1853 which Wood reproduces shows a narrow belt of sugar cultivation about ten miles wide extending from Port of Spain to La Brea along the Gulf of Paria. The remainder of the map is blank except for two or three "settlements" and a small patch of cultivation at Cedros and Mayaro. Two roads are shown leading out from Port of Spain, the first to a short distance beyond Arima and the second to San Fernando with an easterly extension to the "American settlements" in the vicinity of what is today Princes Town. Dotted lines show the bridle paths from Arima to Manzanilla and Toco and from the "American settlements" to Mayaro with a branch to Moruga on the south coast. This was Trinidad at the date of emancipation when the total population was under 80,000 souls of whom 17,000 had been slaves and it was estimated that only one-twentyfifth of the land was under cultivation.

Outside of Port of Spain there was little development during the ensuing years so that when Charles Kingsley visited the island in 1870 (not so very long ago, it was the year of my father's birth) he was paddled through the Caroni swamp in a canoe to visit the "High Woods" which bordered the sugar belt just back of Chaguanas, and he explored the island on horseback along the bridle paths to the Cocal, Blanchisseuse and into the Naparimas. Of his ride into the Naparimas he wrote:

"Being happily for me in the Governor's suite, I had opportunities of seeing the interior of the island which an average traveller could not have, and I looked forward with interest to visiting new settlements in the forests of the interior, which very few of the inhabitants of the island and certainly no strangers had yet seen. . .

"Our journey began by landing on a good new jetty (evidently the terminus of the Eccles tramway at the mouth of the Cipero river) and being transferred at once to the tramway which adorned it. A truck with chairs on it, as usual here, carried us off at a good mule trot, and we ran in the fast fading light through a rolling, hummocky country.

"At last we escaped from our truck and found horses waiting, on which we floundered through mud and moonlight to a certain hospitable house."

A day or two later the party rode on into the Naparimas.

"At one place we seemed to be fairly stopped. We plunged and slid down into a muddy brook, luckily with a gravel bar on which the horses could stand, at least one by one, and found opposite to us a bank of smooth clay, bound with slippery roots, some ten feet high. We looked and looked at it, and the longer we looked — a hunting phrase — the less we liked it. But there was no alternative. Someone jumped off and scrambled up on his hands and knees, his horse was driven up the bank to him — on its knees, likewise more than once — and caught staggering among boughs and mud, and by the time the whole cavalcade was over horses and men looked, as if they had been brick making for a week."

But Kingsley noted signs of progress and the opening up of the land as he rode on "through rich rolling land covered with cane, past sugar-works where crop-time and all its bustle was just beginning, along a tramway which made an excellent horse road and then along one of the new roads which are opening up the yet untouched riches of the island".

Emancipation had, as was to be expected, an immediate effect on the labour market and it was the sugar planters who were the hardest hit by the shortage of labour. It was only natural that the former slaves should associate the hard work of the sugar plantations with their slave status and, with their new found freedom, they sought an easier and more congenial way of life. The result was a general movement of the labour force into the urban and more developed areas. Donald Wood explains the change:

"If the first phase of the settlement of Trinidad was dominated by the sugar planters and to a lesser extent, cocoa farmers who cleared the forest lands along the Gulf of Paria and penetrated into the northern valleys and along the edge of the plain, the second phase in the 1840s was due to free labourers. They founded villages along the line of road and made provision grounds for themselves in easy reach of the estates, sometimes practising a wasteful shifting cultivation that left behind an exhausted soil and a tangle of secondary growth. Some bought, rented, or were given patches of land owned by planters who wished to keep a labour force near at hand. New villages sprang up almost overnight and the neighbourhood of Port of Spain and San Fernando were particularly attractive.

"East of the Dry River in Port of Spain a suburb began to grow, lots were sold in Laventille to form a new settlement. Within five miles of San Fernando, Rambert and Victoria villages were founded soon after 1853. Along the Eastern Main Road to Arima hamlets grew up — Arouca, Tacarigua and D'Abadie, for example — which began the ribbon development that still existed a century later. By 1846 it was believed that 5,400 were living in new villages."

As the result of the urbanising process, the sugar planters were severely hit by the shortage of labour and this was particularly so in the remoter areas of the island.

"As an example," wrote Dr. de Verteuil "once flourishing districts La Brea and Guapo began to decline shortly after emancipation and may be considered now as almost abandoned. In 1840 there were in the district of La Brea seven sugar estates and eleven in Guapo all under the management of their recent proprietors; now only provisions are grown and even these on a reduced scale."

La Brea and Guapo returned to the wilderness. The abandoned sugar mills and their boilers remained to rust and be engulfed by the jungle until they were brought to light again as the oil industry moved in in the 1910s to revitalise the area. Other remote areas like Mayaro suffered the same fate. There had been six sugar estates in this area but as the emancipated slaves moved out these estates were all abandoned.

That the sugar industry was hard hit by the shortage is brought out by the gradual drop in production. In 1838, the crop was 14,312 tons; in 1839, 13,433 tons; in 1840, 12,238 tons, lowest crop for the decade and it was not to start its recovery until indentured East Indian labour was introduced in the 1850's. But what Trinidad lost on the swings of sugar, it gained on the roundabouts of cocoa. Harold Fahey paints this picture of the growth of the cocoa industry:

"By 1821, we find a crop of 1,214,094 lbs and by1851 5,068,923 lbs. In fact, the cocoa industry was becoming more and more popular every year. Under the very humane Spanish slave laws, which the British observed after the capture of the island, a slave was allowed to plant cocoa on the lands allotted to him by law to grow his food. When he raised a thousand cocoa trees to bearing stage he had to be given his freedom. As the sugar industry did not have a similar custom the slave loved the cocoa industry and when freed squatted in some isolated area and formed one of the numerous squatter cocoa estates that existed by 1851 in many isolated areas in Trinidad.

"Political upheavals in Venezuela and the settling of ex-soldiers of the West Indian Regiment in Savanna Grande and Manzanilla also played an important part in bringing Trinidad's production to the five million pounds.

"Alarmed at the popularity of the cocoa industry, the sugar proprietors consistently tried to limit its expansion from the interior of Trinidad by limiting sales of large parcels of land and not granting money to open roads and build bridges, while their representatives on the Legislature used their influence to have a fine costal service from Port of Spain to Cedros and in time to open railway services for the sugar industry. Nothing, however, seemed to be able to check the expansion of the industry, for as a result of revolutions in Venezuela around 1850 many peons had to flee to Trinidad where by the hundreds they squatted in the highwoods of Montserrat and Tamana and formed many fine cocoa estates. With Governor Harris granting these squatters title to their lands a more liberal policy of selling small parcels of land started and hundreds of people of limited means bought ten to fifteen acre blocks and formed estates.

"By 1880, with Trinidad turning out 11,475,530 lbs of cocoa, thousands of acres were yet to come into bearing. When they did we find Trinidad turning out nineteen million pounds in 1893, thirty three million pounds in 1902 and forty one million pounds in 1904. By then it had become the ambition of all classes to own a cocoa estate, and by buying an area of crown lands and the acquiring of small estates bounding it, the large estates were formed, and on Sundays high Government officials, prominent merchants, professional men, shopkeepers and tradesmen could be seen at railway stations, covered with mud, returning from their estates. The chief help asked of Government by all classes of cocoa planters was the building of cart roads, and up to 1880 the Caroni river was still used; some people made fortunes by transporting cocoa in large canoes for the small proprietor while the coastal service transported hundreds of bags of cocoa from the North Coast, Matura, Manzanilla, Mayaro, Moruga and Erin."

Fahey's reference to the slaves' provision gardens and the inducement held out to them to plant cocoa trees in their gardens is of particular interest in that it set the pattern which was to play a major role in the development of the larger cocoa estates after emancipation. This was the development of the "Contract System", under which the estate labourer was granted a small acreage of uncleared land to establish his garden. He cleared the land, and planted his ground provisions, which served the dual purpose of providing ground shade for his young cocoa trees and supplying his needs for ground provisions. At the end of five years the estate owner took over the garden, paying the contractor a fixed fee for every bearing cocoa tree with a sliding scale for the younger trees. The system was beneficial to both parties. The estate owner was able to extend his cultivation at no cost until he took over the garden as a going concern. The contractors were permitted to build their carat covered tapia dwelling on the estate lands thus being available as a source of ready labour. The labourer had his garden and his house and fairly regular work on the estate and received a nice little nest egg at the end of his five-year contract. Most of the larger estates were established and developed on this basis and many of the "fields" or sub-divisions of today's estates bear the names of the contractors who cleared and planted the land.

Fahey's reference to the Venezuelan peons is also of interest as the part which they played in the development of the island is seldom referred to. Fahey places their coming in the 1850s. Donald Wood, however, suggests that they were here before emancipation: "The peons prized their freedom", he tells us, "and were scornful of labour on the sugar estates during the time of slavery.' Wood goes on to explain their origin:

"Of all the immigrants who arrived in the nineteenth century the peons were the best adapted to the frontier conditions of the forest; for they were but an ecological extension of those over the Gulf from which they had been driven by the civil wars. In many ways they were like the buckskin trappers and voyageurs of mixed Amerindian and French descent in the coniferous forests of Quebec. They too, were of mixed race, a new kind of man of Spanish, Negro and Amerindian blood who had been in the making of the of the Latin American tropics for 300 years, and like the men of French Canada they were staunchly Catholic. Both types of pioneer were skilled backwoodsmen, but whereas in Quebec and Lower Canada they were hunters, the peons were predominantly agriculturists, and particularly expert in cultivating one of the native species of the rain forest, cocoa.

. "The greatest gift which the peons brought with them from The Spanish Main was an empirical knowledge of the soils on which cocoa would flourish and the patient skill needed to bring the tree to maturity.

"They moved without fuss into the northern foothills and took up small scale cocoa farming, either on their own account or for Spanish and later French-speaking planters."

They also moved into Montserrat. "Not many years ago," wrote Dr. de Verteuil, "the district or quarter of Montserrat was mostly, if not entirely, occupied by individuals of Spanish descent — peons of the best class who had been lured there by the fertility of the soil and the facility of getting land. Not ten could show any title to the land they occupied".

The peons, while they undoubtedly played a major role in the development of the cocoa industry, also left their mark on the cultural and social environment and the "Spanish" influence which we acknowledge today in our folk music and song — the parang, for instance — originated not from the true Spaniards of the pre-British era but from the Venezuelan peon.

As the cocoa industry took root and flourished during the last quarter of the century, sugar, too, was to stage it's come-back following the introduction of indentured labour in the 1850's, and the granting of land to the East Indians in lieu of their return passages to India. Williams records that between 1885 and 1895, 22,916 acres of crown lands were granted to the Indians and between 1902 and 1912, 31,765 acres and the cane-farming industry was firmly established.

From the small start in the opening up of the country noted by Kingsley in the Naparimas there was a marked agricultural expansion during the last quarter of the century with the opening up of new roads and the establishment of the railway. The railway from Port of Spain to Arima was opened in 1776 and extended to Sangre Grande in 1886 while the line to San Fernando started in 1880 was completed in 1882 and was extended to Princes Town in 1886. The branch line from Cunupia to Tabaquite was laid in 1897.

By the end of the century districts like Manzanilla and Montserrat through which Kingsley had ridden over bush trails were booming with rich cocoa plantations. Of Montserrat, Kingsley had written:

"The Montserrat Hills had been within the last three years almost the most lawless and neglected part of the island. In 1867 there were in Montserrat 400 squatters holding lands of from 3 to 100 acres planted with cocoa, coffee and provisions."

At this stage Government had moved in to regularise the position of the squatters by granting them title to the lands they held. The properties were surveyed, two villages were established one contained the church, the other the Warden's residence and office, the police station and a school. As Montserrat was tamed and word spread of its fertile soils the more wealthy planters moved in to buy up the small holdings and establish their large estates, and by 1895 when my father rode in with his young bride to take charge of one of these estates Montserrat was the stronghold of the French Creole planter.

The development of Manzanilla had followed the same pattern and so by 1904 when I, as a small boy, moved into the district with my parents it was to one of the well-established cocoa plantations which stretched from the rail head at Sangre Grande to the east coast.

CHAPTER VII

MY GENERATION: BOYHOOD DAYS

GREAT grandfather O'Connor married a le Fer, grandfather a Ganteaume de Monteau and father a de Gannes de la Chancellerie and so, when I was brought into the world in 1899, appropriately by the good doctor Ferdinand de Verteuil, there was little doubt as to my French Creole antecedents. I was of the French landowning aristocracy, the privileged class, the social elite. How did that society live and what were the social amenities and privileges which they enjoyed? How do we measure a standard of living? The yardstick is purely relative because with the march of time yesterday's luxuries of the upper class become the accepted necessities of the working class of today. There is little doubt that the average working class family nowadays would hardly accept what we considered as gracious living in my childhood. It is only those of us who have witnessed the transition from the horse-and-buggy to the modem jet airliner and the first motion picture to live television of man's landing on the moon who can fully appreciate the remarkable transformation which has taken place in our way of life.

My children and grandchildren listen with wide-eyed wonderment and a tinge of amusement at the tales of my boyhood; others may find them quaint if not interesting. I was brought up on a cocoa estate and the life which we lived was no doubt typical of other families of my generation. My own life started in the Santa Cruz Valley, then one of the richest cocoa growing areas of the island, but the valley was then a long way off from the civilisation of Port of Spain. The road to Port of Spain lay over the "Saddle" for those in the upper valley with the alternative of going down the valley to take the train from San Juan. This latter route, however, was at times dangerous, if not impassable in the rainy season, as there we no bridges over the river, which crossed the road at several points and I can remember the occasion on which father had his mule swept from under him as he tried to cross the flooded river.

But my earliest and most vivid recollection of the Santa Cruz days is that of being driven late one evening over the Saddle Road into town. I had developed a bad sore throat and my parents feared diphtheria. The nearest doctor was in Port of Spain so I was wrapped in blankets and carried out to the waiting buggy for the long slow drive over the Saddle and down through the Maraval Valley. Luckily, it was not diphtheria but the doctor recommended a fortnight's conversance "down the islands" and it was arranged that I should join cousins who were holidaying at Monos. The island steamer, with its great paddles at either side, was due to leave the lighthouse jetty at 5 a.m. but the cab which had been ordered to take Mother and me to catch the steamer failed to turn up. Mother decided that we would start walking on the chance of picking up a stray cab. The streets were deserted at that early hour except for an old man pushing his hand-cart. Mother explained our predicament, the good Samaritan lifted me on to his hand-cart and we arrived in style as the steamer was about to leave.

From Santa Cruz, the family moved to Manzanilla in 1904. Only a little over thirty years had elapsed since Charles Kingsley had described his journey through the district over almost impassable mud trails through the jungle on his ride to the Cocal, but now Manzanilla was a flourishing cocoa district. The railway had reached Sangre Grande in 1886, a good macadam road led from the village to the east coast and the village of Sangre Grande was thriving on the cocoa prosperity of a wide area. It boasted of, besides the railway station, a post office, police station and court house with several Chinese shops which stocked everything from salt-fish to hardware for the estates.

It was a busy and exciting spot on a Saturday morning as the planters rode or drove in in their buggies to do their week's shopping or to collect their box of groceries which had arrived from Port of Spain by the morning train. Saddle horses were hitched to the posts under the shop galleries and patient mules stood while the estate supplies for the week were being loaded on to their carts.

Our estate was four miles from the village and another four miles beyond lay Manzanilla beach. The house stood back from the main road and was reached by a quarter mile of "gap". The dictionary defines gap as a parting or clearing — is that the origin of our "gap"? It was nothing more, a clearing through the cocoa trees, unpaved, and in the rainy season fetlock deep in mud, and impassable to wheeled traffic. To get to church on a Sunday morning, we walked out to the main road carrying our shoes while the groom led the horse and buggy through the mud accompanied by the yardman carrying buckets of water. We then sat on the wall of the concrete culvert (which incidentally is still there today), washed our feet and put on our shoes before driving off to church.

The amenities and luxuries of estate life were few. The single storey wooden house, located on the hillside, was built to last of native hardwood and cedar. It consisted of two large bedrooms surrounded by a gallery which on two sides had been enclosed and divided into smaller dressing rooms and bedrooms. The other two sides of the gallery were the living rooms. On one side of the house lay the small savannah for the grazing of the cows and mules. To the front, separated by a small garden, lay the two cocoa drying houses and at the back was the kitchen, the servants' quarters, bath house and outoffices. A little way down the hill were the stables. There is no stone or gravel in the Sangre Grande-Manzanilla district, so the yard and paths were unpaved and a sea of mud in the rainy season. Cooking was done on a row of coal-pots in the outside kitchen while the Sunday roast was prepared in the conventional bee-hive mud oven located outside the kitchen door. This oven was heated by stacking firewood inside it. When the fire had burnt itself to embers these were raked out, the meat inserted and the door sealed up.

There was no laid-on water supply. We depended on the four small tanks, one at each corner of the house, to catch the rain from the roof. As the dry season approached, locks were placed on the tanks and bath water was rationed; if the dry season persisted the family moved out to Arima, leaving the last few inches of water in the tanks to see Father through until the rains returned. The labourers and the stock depended for their water supply on the few water holes on the estate and during the dry season these became blacker and blacker with the falling of the immortelle flowers.

Ice was a luxury enjoyed only at the weekend when the estate cart went into the village to fetch the week's groceries which arrived from Port of Spain on the morning train. The fresh meat was packed with a large block of ice which hopefully would last until Sunday. But there was always a supply of cool drinking water from the "drip-stone" or filter. The drip-stone was the equivalent of today's refrigerator. It consisted of two vessels of porous coral set one above the other on a small derrick. The upper vessel was carved out to hold a few buckets of water. The water dripped through the coral vessels, thus becoming filtered, and at the same time cooled by evaporation, into a large earthenware jar at the bottom. On the derrick hung a calabash with a stick through it to serve as a dipper and how cool and fresh that water was.

The "drip-stone" appears to have been an early innovation in Trinidad as Carlton Ottley records:

"When the first Roman Catholic Bishop of the West Indies, Bishop Buckley, arrived in 1820, the Cabildo not only gave him formal welcome on South Quáy,but also provided him with a furnished house in the town. Among the items of furniture which the Cabildo in its wisdom saw fit to provide were the following: One drip-stone for filtering water, four goblets...."

And "goblets", too, were part of our lives — these supplied the cool drinking water inside the house. They were placed on a cool window sill in the pantry and the evaporation of the air on the porous earthenware kept the water delightfully cool. Today's must in every household, the fridge, stacked with cokes and sweet drinks was unknown to us but on special occasions, like birthdays someone might be sent to the main road to intercept the sweet drink cart and we indulged in a case of cola or cream soda.

The marvels of electric light were unknown to us. The kerosene lamps smoked and the candles blew out when it was windy and we sat in darkness many a night. But, perhaps, the greatest hardship was the lack of today's boon to the country dweller: mosquito screens. The house was wide open to every flying insect and in the rainy season these came in their hordes. Mosquitoes and sand flies we took in our stride, but there were the larger flying cockroaches. When one zoomed in and circled the dining room table, there was panic and Mother and the girls ran for the shelter of their mosquito net and we boys had to show our manhood by disposing of the monster.

There were, too, the swarms of rainflies, or "flying ants". When these made their appearance, the only answer was to place the lamp at the far end of the gallery and watch them commit suicide while we sat in the shadow. The black, hard-backed beetle was fun however. We harnessed these with thread to match boxes and organized chariot races along the length of the dining room table. If one's team refused to race, it was decapitated by simply pulling the thread and a new team hitched up. Yes, we were horrid small boys!

Then, too, there was malaria and toothache. Malaria and the horrors of quinine in its raw and bitter state. Children today are dosed on sugar-coated pills and orange flavoured aspirin. We took our quinine raw from a large jar, weighed out in 5 grains by Mother on a small scale and then rolled into a horrid flour-coated pill. The flour coating never worked. Oh, the lingering bitterness of quinine. We had toothache because the nearest dentist was in Port of Spain and the only solace was a wad of cotton wool soaked in laudanum stuck into the cavity.

But it was a good life! We were up early in the morning when there was cocoa to be danced in the drying houses. Then we joined the labourers and sang and danced with them to polish the golden beans with our clean bare up feet, or, father might decide that it was a fine morning to clean up and cutlass the yard. We would that it wake up to the sound of swishing cutlasses and hurry out to join the gang and help to weed the garden. We would then roam through the estate in search of a ripening bunch of bananas on which to set up our trapcage or "lagglee" to catch birds, to find birds' eggs or to add to our collection of butterflies, until we discovered an orange or mango tree under which we could sit and gorge. We might raid one of the contractors' gardens and return laden with juicy stalks of sugarcane to sit on the backsteps and suck cane to our hearts content. In the late afternoon we accompanied the stock-man as he drove his cart into the paragrass field to bring in the bundles of grass for the stables and returned perched precariously on the highly stacked grass.

Occasionally, I accompanied father on his trips to Mayaro where he managed one of grandfather's estates. This was an exciting outing, which had to be fitted in with a low tide as the only "road" was along the beach. The journey was always broken at the Cocal for a drink or lunch with "Boss" Bovell, and to rest the horse. One could not have driven by in any case without availing oneself of the Bovell hospitality.

Then on to the beach again, trotting along until the turn-off through the coconuts to the Nariva Ferry where we rang a large bell to awaken the ferryman from his mid-day nap and he pulled the big ferry over to meet us. We led the horse on to the ferry and watered him as we crossed while father made a deal with the ferryman for a bag of oysters to be picked up on the way back; then back along the beach until the Ortoire ferry and the same procedure, along the narrow track around Point Radix and on to the long sweep of Mayaro beach, to be greeted at last by Aunt Lucy Ganteaume and her daughters.

On one of these trips we ran into a storm. As we came out on to the beach from the Cocal the seas were mountain high and the wind was blowing huge balls of froth from the wave crests up the beach. These drove us further and further up the beach where the going was too soft and the mule could only proceed at a walk. Darkness fell before we crossed the Ortoire ferry and the rain was coming down in driving sheets. Then a large tree across the road held us up for an hour or so until a gang of men cleared a path for us. But Aunt Lucy was up waiting for us with hot chocolate when we eventually arrived.

The Ganteaumes and Mayaro — they were synonymous. Legend has it that a party of Ganteaumes set off from St. Lucia to find El Dorado on the Spanish Main. On the way they overheard their slave crew planning to mutiny and hand their masters over to the French Republican authorities in Martinique. They eliminated the crew, how is not recorded, and sailed on to be finally wrecked the beach at Mayaro where, like the coconuts, they established their roots.

While we life children ran wild and led a wonderfully carefree existence the life led by our parents must have been exceedingly dull by today's standards. Their social circle had a radius of about four miles, a buggy ride. It embraced some six or seven planters, the parish priest, the doctor and the warden. The main social event of the week was the gathering of the Catholic families after Mass on Sunday. Doctor de Gannes' house was near to the church and so it fell to him to provide the rum punches after Mass and here everyone gathered for an hour or so until it was time to drive home for the traditional Sunday lunch of callaloo and crab and fricassée chicken.

On Sunday afternoon a neighbour might drop in for a drink or mother and father would set off in the buggy to pay a call. Sunday was the day for calling as there was sure to be some ice left in the ice box and the men could count on an iced cocktail.

Occasionally Father Dominic would drop in for dinner on Saturday night on his way back from his confessional at Manzanilla to discuss the Irish situation with father or Dr. de Gannes might pass in for lunch if his rounds took him our way. There were occasional overnight visitors when one or other of the Mayaro families journeyed into Port of Spain. They would leave their horse and buggy with us and we would drive them into Sangre Grande to catch the first train on the following morning.

This was the social whirl, a quiet leisurely life when you did not dash past your neighbour on the road at 50 miles per hour but drew up your buggy alongside his for a chat while the horses munched grass on the verge.

There were, however, two outstanding social events of the year, the Catholic Church's harvest festival and the Discovery Day race meeting on the beach. The harvest festival brought new faces into the district as it was traditional, and expected of the gentry, that they should have house guests over the weekend to help swell the coffers of the Church. After High Mass we gathered at the school where bags of cocoa and ground provisions donated by the planters were auctioned for the Church funds. There was a well-stocked bar and lunch was a sumptuous feast as each housewife provided her special dish. There were the ice cream and sweet stalls for the children, stalls with needlework and toys. It was a day to be looked forward to and to be remembered.

The second great event of the year was the Discovery Day race meeting on the beach. Here everyone gathered under the coconuts on their horses, in their buggies, and in the estate carts. Booths were erected and rum flowed freely while the three-card game flourished. There were races for horses, mules, and donkeys. The mules and donkeys, being unpredictable members of the animal kingdom, seldom completed their races, they either bolted into the coconuts or decided to play it cool by swimming out to sea. The highlight of the day's entertainment was, however, invariably supplied by the clerk of the course — the district road overseer. His duty was to clear the course of spectators before each race. This he did by galloping his pony up and down while wielding a formidable hunting crop. It was exceedingly thirsty work and as the day went by his efficiency grew with each of his trips to the bar. By day's end he was far more effective in crowd control than any troop of mounted police.

Life in the other country districts was evidently much the same as ours though with some variations. There is the story of the sugar planter in the Tacarigua district, a bachelor, who always hosted an all-night poker game on Saturday during crop time. After a while his guests noticed that their mules were always tired for the return journey and decided to investigate. During the game one of them sneaked out and, lo and behold! There were the guests' mules being used to rotate the mill to grind his canes!

There is the story, too, of the weekend house party given by a bachelor planter at Mayaro. One of the ladies asked if she could have a bath. "But certainly", replied her host. 'That can be arranged." The bathroom, some coconut palm fronds enclosing a slab of concrete, was pointed out. The lady having undressed, looked around for the water supply when high above her from the coconuts came a deep voice: "A little more to your left, please, lady", and a bucket of water was poured over her by a grinning yardboy.

The men frequently organised a horseback excursion to some place of interest and one such ride was from St. Joseph over the hills to Maracas Bay. It was a long, hard ride and all were exhausted on their return. The party which followed was designed to assuage their thirst and they finally retired to bed in the small hours. Then one member of the party remembered that he was saddle sore. He decided to apply some sticking plasters to where it hurt most. Holding a candle in one hand and with the aid of a large wall mirror he deftly applied the plasters. As he opened his eyes in the morning there was the mirror adorned with sticking plasters.

A PARTY at "Copper Hole" on Monos, 1897

"LA SOLEDAD" at Santa Cruz in 1902. The author's first home. (Spot the author, aged 3).

CHAPTER 8

ON DONKEYS, MULES AND HORSES

THERE were, undoubtedly, compensations for the young in the horse and buggy days. One did not have to await the ripe old age of eighteen before getting a licence to drive Dad's car. There were donkeys, mules and horses in the stables and these were there for the saddling. We were not taught to ride, but by natural evolution went from the toddler stage into the saddle. It started with Polly, a small woolly baby donkey that arrived one morning. Polly was christened after Pretty Polly who had won the One Thousand Guineas and The Oaks in 1904 so that she must have arrived in 1905. At that date I was six years old and the eldest of four boys and Polly was to have a hard time with four masters!

To start with, some well-meaning relative had given us a tricycle, but as the gap and yard were unpaved there was nowhere to ride it. The solution was to harness Polly to it and have her pull us through the muddiest paths and up the steepest grades we could find. The tricycle did not last long. Then we found a discarded bath tub — one of those nice round flat ones with handles on it. This became a beautiful sledge in which Polly could haul us through the mud. Polly was hitched up and we yelled "Gee-up", luckily before anyone had got aboard. As Polly obediently moved off, there was a clang, and terrified, she broke into a gallop. The noise increased and Polly panicked, the bath tub bumped higher and higher until luckily the rope parted as Polly disappeared into the cocoa. It was several days before we found her!

But we were not daunted. Four of us could not ride Polly at once so we had to have a buggy. Our chance came when we found two wheels and an axle from a discarded "two wheel gig." We bound a piece of two-by-four to the axle to which we nailed a seat and two bamboo shafts. A set of harness was contrived from bits and pieces from the saddle-room and Polly was installed between the shafts. Now we had our own means of transport and could travel far afield, at least two miles from home.

The only restriction placed on our journeys was that of having to be home before dark, but there was the occasion on which we lost count of time, as small boys are wont to do, and darkness was already upon us before we started for home. Polly had had one of her hard days and decided that to trot was beyond her. There was still a mile to go in the inky darkness when we heard the welcome sound of a galloping horse coming towards us, and four very frightened small boys were escorted home by a relieved father who had come in search of us.

There were periods, however, when Polly had it easy. These were the occasions when we decided that she should have a baby. We had not yet learnt of the birds and the bees and were convinced that all that was necessary was a good bed of straw and lots of oats. Polly was accordingly installed while we raided the oats barrel and left her to enjoy a rest for a few days. When nothing happened, however, the call of the road became too strong and poor Polly was back in harness.

From Polly we progressed to the estate horses and mules, a varied assortment on which we could travel farther afield. When father and mother went calling in their buggy we accompanied them as outriders. We rode to school, to church, to see our friends, but mostly just for the fun of it. We galloped on the macadam main road and explored the unpaved side roads for a good stretch on which to race against each other.

There was little traffic on the roads but what there was interesting and picturesque. There were the estate carts piled high with bags of cocoa with its large sleek mule between the shafts and two small ones as leaders in tandem. The driver took pride in his team; his reins were threaded through hundreds of steel rings fixed to the mules' harnesses and these jingled as he tugged at his reins. These rings were a definite status symbol with every cart driver, together with his long whip which he could crack like a rifle shot or flick a fly from his lead mule's ear. Then there was the Syrian peddler with his cedar box of cheap jewellery slung over his shoulder followed by his East Indian porter with a huge bundle of cotton piece goods on his head. They walked the roads from estate to estate to set up shop under the shade of a mango tree near the pay office.

On turning the next corner, we would see a lone horseman and recognise our clerk of the course of race days. a lone It is pay day so he would be very drunk and had dropped his prized riding crop. His steed is circling the whip and he is leaning over precariously in the saddle in the hope that his magnetic gaze will effect a miracle. We would dismount, hand him his treasure and gallop off with him and leave him safely in the next rum shop.

As we galloped along we would overtake a party of sweating porters taking a "sick" to the doctor's. A hammock is slung on a long bamboo pole. Under each end of the pole is a strong man's shoulder as they hurry along at a jog-trot. The "sick" is in the hammock and several other relief porters jog alongside and still on the jog the hammock is passed over to these reliefs. They have come out from some side road and are covered with mud, but they have been on the jog for many miles and still have two miles to cover; but the sick must be got to the doctor and the days of the taxi and the motor ambulance are a long way off.

Other memories come back to me: It is early morning and I have been up at dawn to drive father to the first train in the two wheel gig. The air is crisp and the mare is skittish as we fly along at a brisk trot when around the bend the bread van is seen approaching. We flag it down and buy two one-cent loaves of hot fresh bread. The village is waking as we rush through Sangre Grande and hear the shrill whistle of the engine to signal the departure of the train but all is well; The station master has seen us and he will never wave his green flag until Mr. Taffy is safely on board. I turn the mare and drive back through the village feeling very important alone in the gig with a high stepping mare.

One of our favourite rides was to the steamer depot at the mouth of the Lebranche River where the coastal steamer called on its round-the-island trip from Tobago. Here passengers were brought ashore in the ship's surf boats with pigs, goats and chickens and there was always the chance that a Tobago pony would be swam ashore. But there was the dreadful morning on which we heard that one of the surf boats had been swamped in the heavy surf many had been drowned. Father galloped off to the beach and spent many gruesome hours helping to recover bodies from the sea.

Rochie Field was our nearest neighbour. He was a keen racing man and generally had a horse or two in training. We naturally longed for a chance to ride a real race horse but when this came I was utterly disgraced. We had ridden to Manzanilla beach to see Rochie exercise his string. His exercise boy did not turn up and he offered me the mount. I was lifted into the saddle with instructions to go down to a certain point and let my mount come back freely. This was the biggest horse I had ever been on. I was ten years old and weighed about 60 lbs. I was a long way off the ground and there was an awful lot of horse under me, but I was full of confidence. Or reaching my marker, a stump on the beach, I would take a firm hold, tum, stop and break from a standing start when I quite ready. But this was a race horse. As I touched him with my heel he pivoted on one hind leg and bounded into the air with the longest stride in the history of horse flesh. Panic seized me, I gathered my reins and pulled for all I was worth but to no avail. I would never stop this monster, and there was a good five miles to his stable.

As I passed Rochie I yelled out that I could not stop, but my mount had had his gallop and knew his distance. As I rode back to Rochie, his 200 lbs. were shaking with laughter. I felt I had a lot to live down. Today, I can console myself with the thought that the exercise lad whose place I had taken was to develop into one of our leading jockeys and later into one of our most successful trainers, the late Johnny Marcelle. I could hardly have emulated him.

My proudest moment on horseback was when I commanded the mounted guard of honour for the reception of the Governor, Sir George Le Hunt, on the occasion of his first official visit to the district. This mounted guard of honour consisted of the four O'Connor brothers, Earl Lickfold and Willie Robinson. We had spent the week grooming our mounts and polishing our saddlery. As the Governor dismounted from his carriage, I called the cavalry detachment to order and saluted. The Governor solemnly inspected us and congratulated us on the smart turnout. This was no doubt the youngest guard of honour ever mounted for a colonial governor!

Another memorable occasion was the day on which we made off with the Archbishop's buggy. His Grace was in the district for the weekend for a confirmation ceremony. Our parish priest, to impress His Grace, or perhaps lacking confidence in his local talent, invited several St. Mary's College boys for the weekend to serve as altar boys. After High Mass at Manzanilla, His Grace was being entertained at lunch while we boys were left on our own. It seemed natural that, as hosts, we should show off our beach, only two miles away, to the boys from town. It seemed only natural too, that we should provide the best means of transport. This was naturally the buggy which had been placed at the disposal of His Grace. Several hours later, eight small boys running naked on the beach after their swim, were rounded up by two irate priests. It was, I am sure, only the humour of the Irish clergy that saved us from a sound thrashing.

Riding was fun until the motor bus descended us. No one in the district yet had a motor car, but we had heard that such things existed and that there were a few on the island. Then suddenly and without warning, the bus was upon us. This was the noisiest and smelliest of contraptions which scared the daylight out of us. It was supposed to run a regular schedule between the railway and Manzanilla twice a day. We now tried to schedule our rides to miss the bus, but this was impossible to achieve owing to its frequent breakdowns. We would hear that the bus had broken down, and with joy set of on our mounts only to ride headlong into it at the first turn of the road — the beastly thing had been repaired — our mounts would either dash into the cocoa or turn and head for home ahead of the monster until we could turn off into some side road. That bus must have helped in a great way to improve our horsemanship.

The pride and joy of our stables was and will always remain "Shamrock", who was my very own. Rochie Field brought him into the yard early one morning. Shamrock stood thirteen hands two inches, was a chestnut roan, and had the configuration of a thoroughbred. He was the most beautiful thing that a small boy could have seen. Father bought him on the spot and in part payment Rochie received Polly for his small daughter. Shamrock was as gentle as a kitten and as light on his legs. Shortly thereafter we decided to enter him for the Agriculture show of 1912 to compete in the open jumping competition. We laid down some cart loads of sand on the gap, built a hurdle and Shamrock was in training for the great event. He proved a natural jumper and we felt confident that we had the challenge cup in the bag. But Father, being a perfectionist, was not satisfied. Shamrock must not only be, but must look the part of a champion. All the estate supply of oats was diverted to him, he started to "feel his oats" and by the time we got him into town for the big event he was quite unmanageable! In the Princes Building grounds, instead of facing his jumps, he stood on his hind legs and waved at the crowds. In despair, I gave up and handed over to my younger brother who was more of a 'rough-rider" than I was, and to the cheers of the crowd Shamrock finally took his jumps and won the cup.

Alas! Shamrock had to be sold a few months later to pay my fare when I was sent off to school in Ireland.

THE author on "Shamrock" in 1911

THE family set off for a picnic on Manzanilla Beach. Note father's attire.

"LA MARIQUITA" at Manzanilla. The "New House" was built in 1916.

THE Estate House with Cocoa House in foreground.

The Author in 1918.

CHAPTER IX

A VISIT TO PORT OF SPAIN

AS children our visits to Port of Spain were few and far between; perhaps once or twice a year, but always an adventure. There was the excitement of getting up before dawn to catch the first train, then the thrill of the train journey as we installed ourselves in the second class coach and eagerly looked out at each stop to see who would be joining us. There was always the prospect of cousins meeting us at Guaico, Arima or Tunapuna. We were impressed by the speed of the train, and the tales we heard that in England trains ran at a mile a minute — what a fantastic speed! Would we ever get up to that?

On arrival in Port of Spain there was the line of cabs awaiting the incoming train and we hoped that David would be there — Ah! — there he was. David had been father's groom in the Santa Cruz days and he had received a bullet in his shoulder during the Water Riots of 1903. Father, as a member of the Light Horse, had been called out during the riots and David had received a stray bullet while standing by with his master's horse. Now he was a cabby and our childhood hero and he always had to bare his shoulder to show us his bullet wound as he drove us up to St. Ann's where we usually stayed with relatives when in town. The large house on Church Avenue is still there just below the Catholic Church.

Church Avenue was then the northern limit of the town and the terminus of the tram line so that in staying there we had the best of two worlds. In the early mornings we would set off with our butterfly nets in search of Blue Emperors up the St. Ann's and Cascade rivers. We would stop at the tram terminal to see the conductor reverse the boom on the top of the tram for the return trip to town and marvel at how adept he was in contacting the overhead wire at first go. We would gaze across the river at the Coblentz House with its enormous expanse of gardens. I remember the afternoon on which I sauntered down alone to watch the trams come and go. I was loaded with a beautiful stock of new marbles which I had acquired on Frederick Street that morning and challenged by a little black boy to pitch for keeps. Within half an hour my marbles were all gone.

On Sunday afternoon we would be dressed in our best sailor-suits and escorted by our nurse to listen to the band in Government House Gardens and watch the fine ladies being driven around the Savannah in their carriages or if we were lucky we were each given six cents for a tram ride on the savannah car which circled the Queen's Park inside the railings. This was a special treat, cool and invigorating as you speeded along, with the bell clanging to scare the grazing cows off the track and the hope that one would be caught on the "cow catcher" which protruded from the front the tram. On the other hand if we felt very adventurous we would take the tram down to Park Street and transfer to the east-west line for the run through St. James to the sea breeze of Cocorite and on to far off Four Roads.

As a special treat we would be taken to the Fire Brigade station where the gleaming harness hung over the shafts of the fire engines ready to be dropped on to the beautiful horses which were trained to trot out of their stalls at the sound of the alarm bell.

But the greatest treat of all was to be in town for the races when father took me to the stand with him in the heyday of "Sailor" and his great Barbadian rival, "Houton". The Governor arrived with his lady in an open carriage with his mounted escort, the Police Band played during the intervals and father took me with him into the paddock to see the horses saddled and to chat with the jockeys and trainers.

One of my more memorable visits to Port of Spain was for the celebration of King George the Fifth's coronation. There was, of course, a race meeting and there were to be fire-works in the Savannah in the evening to which we were all looking forward. On this occasion we children did not go to the Grand Stand for the races but perched on the wall of the Peschiers cemetery. In midafternoon, however, the heavens opened and, drenched to the skin, we had to race for "home", on this occasion upper St. Vincent Street, where we spent the rest of the day praying for the rain to stop. It cleared slightly and about 7 p.m. there was a boom and a rocket lit the sky. The fire-works were on and we raced for the Savannah but alas, there were no fire-works. All had been destroyed by the afternoon rain!

No visit to Port of Spain would have been complete a morning shopping on Frederick street, for fittings of new sailor suits, those stiffly starched banes of a small boy's life in my early youth, and new shoes for the impending Christmas holidays. We would take an early morning tram from St. Ann's, and alight at Glendinning's but Frederick Street was a very different picture in those far-away days. Apart from the trams and the clip-clop- of horse-drawn carts, there was little traffic on the street. The pavement was almost an exclusive club were the upper classes met, chatted and shopped. The working classes could not afford to shop in this area and they did not trespass on the preserves of the gentry. Of course, there were no such things as "limers", no oddly garbed tourists, so shopping was a leisurely and social outing, where one met one's equals and friends, to end up eventually at the Swiss Patisserie for delicious cream cakes.

Visits to town were not all fun and games, however. The social amenities had to be complied with. These consisted of having to pay our respects to innumerable old aunts and uncles. Dressed in our best and accompanied by our parents we took a cab and went "calling" to be patted on the head and told how we had grown since last visit. We then sat stiffly in the drawing room while the elders chatted in French so that we would not understand while the gossip!

Was this the start of a generation gap? It is curious that while French was spoken fluently by my parents' generation — they were all bilingual — they made no attempt to pass it on to our generation but used it rather to exclude us from their secrets! Perhaps, the dropping of French by our generation was the first phase of the waning of the French influence which had dominated our society for over a hundred years.

One visit that we always enjoyed, however, was to old Uncle Felix, a bachelor and the last of the second generation of O'Connors in Trinidad. He took snuff from a silver snuff box which fascinated us and his flowing white beard was stained a golden yellow. His house was a veritable museum, the walls hung with a large brass blunderbuss, duelling pistols and swords and his backyard was full of pigeons. He died in 1911 at the age of 83 and it is to his acquisitiveness that I owe the family papers that have come down to me.

Another highlight of visits to Port of Spain was to watch Carnival from "The Hermitage". This was the walled-in residence of Mr. Freddie Scott which stood at the corner of Tragarete Road and St. Vincent Street – now the site of the Battoo Brother's complex. It was then an exclusive school for young ladies run by the Misses Scott which my sister attended. "The Hermitage" was an ideal vantage point from which to view the revelry. We could look over the high wall, see it all and yet be apart from it for Carnival in my boyhood was a wild and vulgar affair and we were not allowed out on the streets. From the high wall, however, we could look down on it in safety — the jab-jabs, the stick fights, the Red-Indian bands - a long way off from the organised bands of today, but it was Carnival and uninhibited.

CHAPTER X

SCHOOLING

AT this stage the reader might well be wondering where and how we fitted in any schooling. This was varied and somewhat sporadic. Presumably, mother had taught us our ABC and the fact that two and two make four, but I can recall no set pattern or regular hours. There is a dim memory of a part-time governess, a young teacher from the Manzanilla Primary Schooling, but not until Mrs. Lickfold "adopted" me did I start my education.

Jack Lickfold managed Santa Estella Estate two miles away from us. His wife was a gifted teacher, and their son Earl was just my age, so Mrs. Lickfold suggested that I share my lessons with him. For about two years I galloped off to Santa Estella each morning on one of the estate mules or horses. Our main text book was Arthur Mee's Children's Encyclopedia, and to this wonderful publication and to Hilary Lickfold I owe an enduring debt of gratitude.

But Earl was sent off to boarding school in England and again there was an educational crisis. The good Father Dominic, however, filled the gap by recommending one of his young teachers. In exchange for a room on the estate, this young man gave us an hour's schooling each morning before setting off for his school on his bicycle. He would leave us our homework and return in the evening for another two hours. Then Father Dominic came to our rescue again. He founded the Sangre Grande High School as an annex to his parish school to cater for the dozen or so sons and daughters of the principal shopkeepers of the village who could presumably pay a small fee for the "higher education" of their children. So I rode each morning to the High School and stabled my mount at the Presbytery. The High School was located in a corner of the primary school building and during the lunch break we "spun top" or played marbles and mixed freely with the boys from the primary. But time was running out and in

August 1912 at the age of 13 I set sail for Ireland "to further my education."

At Clongowes Wood College in its beautiful setting of woods and surrounded by acres of the greenest turf playing fields, I learned the history of Ireland — that Sir Ralph Abercrombie had acted as a perfect gentleman in his conquest of Trinidad compared with his treatment of the Irish when he governed them, that the Irish peasant had been, and still was, far worse off than the working classes in Trinidad, that thousands had died of starvation during the potato famine while other thousands had emigrated to America under conditions comparable or worse to those experienced during the slave trade or East Indian immigration.

I was shocked, too, by the pinched red faces of the poor little urchins in the streets of Dublin shivering in the cold, and came to realise that Trinidad with its sunshine was indeed a land of milk and honey. I was in Ireland, too, to witness the suppression of the 1916 Easter uprising, as bloody suppression as was that of the Jamaica uprising of 1865. I quote these facts merely to emphasise that man's inhumanity to man has been universal and is not unique to any country, time nor race.

I was caught in Ireland by the First World War and on leaving school in 1917, joined the Army as everyone else was doing, but was lucky in that my cadetship in an officer's training corps extended beyond the Armistice and so I was saved from the horrors of trench warfare. It was August 1919 before I got back to Trinidad and how different it was to the land I had left seven years before!

The horse and buggy had been replaced by the motor car; Cipriani was preaching "Democracy" and the rights of the barefoot poor, and the oil industry was established. The price of cocoa had been good during the war years and a new two-storied house had been built on our estate. An era had ended and a new one was unfolding.

CHAPTER XI

LA CHANCE

MY maternal grandfather Joseph Gaston de Gannes was the last of the patriarchs and his country home, La Chance, near Arima was paradise to us children. But La Chance was more than that. It was the realisation of the dreams of an indomitable pioneer and it was part of the history of Trinidad at the turn of the century. La Chance typified the old order of the French Creole with its accent on close family life and gracious living which had been the hallmark of colonial New Orleans from whence the de Gannes had sailed to the Caribbean. The fortunes of the French families in Trinidad had fluctuated over the years but with the re-birth of the cocoa industry in the 1890s they were again in the ascendency and La Chance was a symbol of the renaissance.

Tracing their ancestry back to the Dukes of Brittany in the days of the Crusades, the de Gannes were among our founding fathers. They were one of the aristocratic French families who helped to build the French empire in the New World. Settling first in New Orleans they moved to Martinique and then to Grenada where they were rich and had many slaves. In Martinique Rose de Gannes married Roume de Saint Laurent and her son Rose Roume de Saint Laurent founded the French colony in Trinidad.

On his arrival in Trinidad Saint Laurent obtained from Governor Chacon the grant of some 600 acres in the Maraval valley for his mother. She followed him to Trinidad, and having become a widow married a Spanish officer, the Marquis de Charras. Her estate, called Champs Elysées, embraced what is today the St. Andrew's Golf Club and the Country Club and here Madame de Charras lived and was buried in the grounds of the Country Club. The estate then passed to her brother Chevalier de Gannes and later to the de Boissiere family.

An interesting footnote to the history of Champs Elysees is that Sir Ralph Woodford had attempted to purchase the estate from the de Gannes as the site for Government House. The family was asking $75,000 for the property but Woodford had hopes that he could acquire it for $45,000. He was, however, unable to obtain the necessary grant from the Home Government and the deal fell through.

Gaston de Gannes was the grandson of one of Madame de Charras' brothers. He was born in 1838 and by the time he had grown up the fortunes of the family had declined, as had that of many another family, following on Emancipation. The price of cocoa was at its lowest, but undaunted he undertook the management of his father's estates to become one of the pioneers in the rebirth of the cocoa industry. In the late 1860s he married Miss Sophie Cipriani and took his young bride up the Caroni by corial (dug-out canoe) where on the banks of the river just south of the village of Arima he built his cocoa empire.

Doctor de Verteuil has left us this picture of the Caroni in those days:

> "For years the Caroni river was the real highway to Port of Spain. It is in this Ward (Upper Caroni) that the Guanapo and Aripo join to form the Caroni; half a mile lower down it received the Tumpuna. The banks of the Caroni are high and steep; its course extremely winding. After its junction with the Tumpuna the depth of water varies from one to three feet down to the point reached by the tidal flow, and from four to twelve feet below that point to its outflow. The shallow mud bar at its mouth can only be crossed at high tide. The mean time descending in a corial from Tumpuna to the sea is eight hours, but going up, or against the current is very tedious as the canoe is pushed by a long pole."

Can we imagine the feelings of the young bride during her day long trip up the river to her new home, her hopes and fears as she was helped ashore on the muddy banks as dusk was falling? But this was the spirit and the courage that built Trinidad.

In this far off spot (the nearest habitation was the village of Arima six miles to the north over a muddy mule trail, or a day's journey down river to Port of Spain), Gaston de Gannes founded his cocoa empire and raised a large family. As he prospered, he extended his empire into Guaico, Manzanilla and as far afield as

Mayaro, and then as his family was growing up he moved nearer to civilisation in the shape of the growing town of Arima which became linked by the railway with Port of Spain. In Arima, he acquired 50 acres on the O'Meara Road just south of the railway station and there built La Chance.

As I remember La Chance in my boyhood it was an enormous two-storied house with at least eight or ten large bedrooms. The long mahogany table in the dining room sat twenty or more and was flanked by two huge oil paintings, the work of the daughters of the house. One was a still life of English fruit, the other of our local fruit. There was the spacious drawing room with its two great floor- to-ceiling mirrors facing each other which reflected and multiplied the glittering chandelier over and over again so that we children tried to count, but never could, the infinite reflections of the diminishing lights. The grand piano stood in one corner of the room and the floors were impeccably waxed and polished.

The great house stood back about a hundred yards from the road and was approached by two gravel driveways which curved and met under a covered portico from which marble steps led up to the front gallery. Grandfather had ensured that he would not be over-built. The house was surrounded by extensive pastures for the grazing of his cows, there were stables and coach houses and servants' quarters, but our favourite spot as small boys was the huge cow pen into the rafters of which we climbed to watch the cows come in to be milked. Across the road lay the orange orchard through which ran a clear stream on the banks of which was the fascinating rampump which supplied water to the entire establishment.

As children, we spent a great deal of time at La Chance. Any excuse took us there for days or weeks — the school holidays, the Santa Rosa Races or when our water supply failed at Manzanilla were all good reasons to descend on La Chance. Grandfather loved to have his family around him and La Chance had been built with that end in view. But New Year's Day was his special day. It was the accepted tradition, and as imperative as a royal command, that all his children with their respective husbands and wives and children, to say nothing of the nannies and nurse-maids should gather for the great day, and I doubt if there was a son-in-law or daughter-in-law who would have dared to be absent on any excuse.

Some families took up residence from before Christmas while others came only for the day. For those of us in residence, the days before the great day were filled with excitement. A large Christmas tree could be seen through the windows of one of the ante-rooms which was kept securely locked as the grown-ups busied themselves decorating the tree and labelling the presents, and we tried to peep through the key hole to see which was to be ours. The boys explored the estate or ran races up and down the driveways and the little girls played house with their dolls. Then the big day arrived. We were up at dawn to wish Grandpa a happy New Year. He would be standing in his bedroom near his huge wardrobe with its doors open, as on the inside was tacked a neatly written list of grandchildren. As we all paraded in and out with our good wishes, he would consult his list and hand out the appropriate largesse. A golden sovereign to the eldest son of each family, a half-sovereign to the eldest girl and a silver crown or half crown down the line to the younger children. The golden sovereign was soon to be a thing of the past!

Then to breakfast of hot chocolate and fresh bread and off to dress for nine o'clock Mass in Arima. When dressed, the little boys in their stiffly starched white sailor suits, the older ones with their jackets and Eton collars, he girls in their bonnets and large hair ribbons, were all marshalled on the front steps to await the line of carriages and cabs for the drive to Arima. Leading the procession would be Grandpa and Grandma's imposing carriage drawn by its pair of imported matched bays, Nellie and Daisy. Old Dotting sat stiff and upright on the high driver's seat, and it was a special honour for the two grandsons who were selected to sit beside him. Then followed the line of cabs supplied by the John Brothers of Arima. By some unknown feat of organisation and communication the John Brothers always knew exactly how many cabs were needed at La Chance. Be it for Mass on Sunday or Holiday, for the Santa Rosa races, or to take one or more families to catch a train, the Johns were there on time and in sufficient numbers.

On our return from Mass, first the children were fed in a marquee erected on the front lawn, and what a feast it was. Then we were turned loose as the grown-ups took their places at the long table in the dining room with Grandpa at the head of the table proudly surveying his brood. The red and white wines which imported directly from France in their casks and which had carefully bottled and laid down in the cellar under Grandpa's supervision, were now expertly served by St. Hill the butler, as much of an institution as everything else in the house-hold.

On looking back I can only marvel at how La Chance on New Year's Day, 1912, which was to be my last before going off to school in Ireland, there were fifty-four grandchildren assembled and yet, as I recall it, the household staff consisted of Hill, the butler, a cook somewhere in the background and dear old Jane, Grandma's personal maid. Each family, of course, brought along its own nannies and nurse-maids and presumably gave a general hand, but the multitude was housed and fed and transported to Church while Grandma sat serenely in her rocker in the large bow-window of her bedroom with apparently not a worry in the world!

When the grown-ups had finished their lunch, it was time to gather around the Christmas tree for the distribution of presents.

Dinner in the evening for the grown-ups was as grand and as lunch had been, but as some of the families had returned after lunch, a few of the older children who were in residence might be honoured with a place at the big table. This was indeed an honour but you had to be on your very best behaviour. The reward was a colouring of Claret in your glass of water. On the other hand, if you did not rate a seat at the big table you might be permitted to sit up for the gathering in the drawing room after dinner. This was the occasion of family talent on parade. The teenaged girls played their set pieces on the grand piano and the boys did recitations. I was a hit with *The Assyrian Came Down Like a Wolf On The Fold*. Then one of the aunts would sit at the grand piano while all joined in the choruses of the latest popular songs.

Grandpa was a disciplinarian and very much of the old school. Children were to be seen and not heard — two things were taboo, one was whistling in the house ("If you want to whistle go to the stables!") the other was running through the house. I know he loved us all dearly but we were somewhat awed by him as he could wither a small boy with a glance or his sharp, "You, Sir!" His pride and joy were his Julie mango trees and, perhaps, our awe of the old gentleman is best expressed by the fact that no small boy ever dared to pick one of his mangoes! He was a grand and imposing figure, with his neatly trimmed white beard, as he strode about his domain and at seventy-four could still take the morning train to Sangre Grande to descend upon us by cab, walk for hours through the estate, and return home in the evening.

Another big weekend at La Chance was for the Santa Rosa races. Uncle Joe's house was on the south side of the Arima savannah and this was our grandstand. We crossed the road and were on the rails to see our favourites "Ben Battle" and "Little Diamond" race by. Then, too, there was polo to be watched on Sunday afternoons when the planters from the surrounding districts descended on the Savannah in their buggies and the grooms brought in the ponies. The ladies sat in their buggies and we children wandered through the small crowd admiring the ponies and feasting on ice cream and cakes from the vendors, but the "Special" of Arima polo was the Lavanie man! "Lavanie" was an Arima institution and the friend of all children. On his tray of sweets he had a small roulette wheel; for one cent you spun the wheel and scored one, two or three of his delicious sticks of peppermint, aniseed or other wonderful flavour!

The price we pay for progress. The motor car replaced the planters' ponies and so polo in Trinidad died. A walled-in velodrome has replaced the Arima polo ground and race-track.

It was from La Chance too that I saw the first movie to be shown in Trinidad. This was the Passion Play, appropriately shown on Good Friday, in the open air on the Arima savannah. It was an occasion not to be missed, so we journeyed to La Chance for the weekend, and all, young and old, were solemnly and suitably impressed.

But like the silent, flickering movie, La Chance, too, has gone. The O'Meara savannah over which we roamed so freely is now an industrial estate; grandfather's pastures have disappeared under a housing development and the rose garden at the back of the great house will go down in local history, not as part of a gracious home, but as the site of the gruesome Malik murders. *Sic transit gloria mundi.*

"LA CHANCE" in its hey-day. The home of Gaston De Gannes.

CHAPTER XII

THE OIL AGE

AT the turn of the century, there could have been few who envisaged the coming of the Oil Age and fewer who could have foreseen the tremendous impact which it was to have on the future of mankind. The oil age might be considered as having been conceived in the 1860s when the first oil wells were drilled in Baku, Russia, and Pennsylvania in the United States, but it was not until 1908 that the first rumblings of its impending birth reverberated around the world as the D'Arcy Exploration Company struck its spectacular gusher at Majid-i-Salaman in Persia.

Then, as the vast potential began to enfold, the genius of Winston Churchill ordered the conversion of the British Navy from coal to oil fuel and the shock of the 1914 war precipitated the birth of the oil age.

In 1959, the British Petroleum Company published *B.P., Fifty Years in Pictures* to mark the half century anniversary of the Majid-i-Salaman discovery and the caption to one of its pictures reads: "The 1914 war started with horses but halfway through the petrol engine arrived." To those of us who witnessed the change what vivid memories that caption recalls, especially to those of us in Trinidad. For, in Trinidad too, the oil age had been in the throes of its birth pains for many years and the war was to stimulate the birth and growth of our lusty infant.

Raleigh had discovered our Pitch Lake, Admiral Cochrane in 1850 had been impressed with its potential as a source of fuel for the British Navy — "Could this pitch be rendered applicable (as fuel), our vessels would be supplied when an enemy would be almost deprived of the use of steam in these parts" — and Charles Kingsley had stumbled over the remains of our first oil well as he walked across the La Brea peninsula in 1870. His description and comments are worth quoting:

"We hurried on along the trace, which now sloped rapidly downhill. Suddenly, a loathsome smell defiled the air. Was there a gas house in the wilderness? Or, had the poles of Paradise been just smeared with bad coal-tar? Not exactly, but across the path crept, festering in the sun, a black runnel of petroleum and water, and twenty yards to our left under a fast crumbling trunk what was a year or two ago a little engine house, now roof, beams, machinery, were all tumbled down and tangled in hideous and somewhat dangerous ruin over a shaft in the middle of which a rusty pump cylinder gurgled and clicked and bubbled and spewed with black oil and nasty gas; a foul ulcer in dame Nature's side which happily was healing fast beneath the tropic rain and sun. The creepers were climbing over it, the earth crumbling into it and in a few years more the whole would be engulfed in forest and the oil-spring it is to be hoped, choked up with mud".

Kingsley saw it as "the remnant of one of the many rash speculations connected with the Pitch Lake," but how many more rash speculations were to follow in its wake before Kingsley's hope "that these treasures of heat and light should not remain forever locked up and idle in the wilderness". Less than 40 years later, in fact, they were finally unlocked, the oil age was born and with it a new and exciting era opened up for Trinidad.

Dr. Williams in his *History of the People of Trinidad and Tobago,* writes:

"By the end of the war, three major changes had taken place in Trinidad. The first was the discovery of oil in commercial quantities in 1910, and Trinidad, producing sugar which was of little interest to the British Board of Trade became an oil colony of enormous importance to the British Admiralty. The output of crude barrels of oil increased from 125,112 barrels in 1910 to 2,083,027 barrels in 1920."

It would appear that to him the birth of the oil age in Trinidad had merely political connotations: we "became of enormous importance to the British Admiralty". He appeared not to be impressed that we had entered a new and exciting era, an era which was to have a profound impact on each and every one of us. But perhaps it is only those of us who witnessed its birth and were part of the environment into which it was born who can fully appreciate and understand the explosive changes which the oil industry brought about in our social and economic life. The younger generation see the picture as it is today without realising that when oil was discovered during the first decade of the century Trinidad was an undeveloped land, and this was particularly so in the southern areas where the oil potential lay. Vast areas of forest were unexplored; roads were sparse or non-existent; we were still in the horse and buggy age; the amenities of life were few and far between; malaria was rampant and there was the ever-present fear of yellow fever. The labour force, based purely on agriculture, was unskilled and there was no artisan or professional class on which the new industry could draw.

It was against this background that the oil industry was born and struggled towards maturity. Foreign personnel ranging from artisans to professional engineers had to be brought in. These had to be provided with housing and the basic comforts of life where none existed. Thus the oil camps were established and these, as we shall see, were to have profound effects on the social scene.

Initially, the oil camps were isolated from each other and from the local communities by long distances and bad roads and, consisting almost entirely of expatriates, it was only natural that they developed into close knit communities depending entirely on their own resources for their physical and social needs. They had little in common with the few planters and government officials scattered over the area. The business community in San Fernando had little to offer them and Port-of-Spain was a very long way off over almost impassable roads. As the industry grew and the camps expanded they provided their own clubhouses and other recreational facilities for their members and these had the effect of making them even more self-contained and separate from the general community.

In their isolation, however, the oil camps set a new trend in rural development and housing. Perhaps, their greatest contribution in the early days was the introduction of the mosquito proof bungalow to combat the ravages of malaria; they introduced electric light into areas of darkness and established pipe-borne water where none had existed, and as the years went by they extended these facilities to the neighbouring communities which sprang up on the outskirts of the camps. They established medical services in areas far removed from the reach of the district medical officers. The social impact of the oil camps can be seen today in such townships as Point Fortin and Marabella which have grown, from a few tapia huts into thriving communities with their supermarkets, banks, cinemas and secondary schools.

There was, however, one aspect of camp life which had unfortunate repercussions. By the nature of their self-containment the social and working environments of the staff camps were inseparable and this led to the almost total exclusion of coloured personnel from staff positions in the industry. To understand and appreciate the nuances of this situation, however, one must, as in the case slavery and labour, view it in the context of the times and the social structure that pertained. Unfortunately, in the twenties and even in the thirties, the Trinidadian society had not yet attained the social integration of which we boast today. There had been little change in outlook since 1858 when "Collegatarius", quoted in an earlier chapter, had complained in the local Press that the white man only treated the coloureds as familiar equals during business discussions but outside the "mart" human relations dried up. Therein lay the problem: the coloured element, excluded from the club house on ethnic grounds, was debarred from staff positions. This is now ancient history but if the coloured element still harbours any resentment at the discrimination meted out to it in the early days of the industry, it may be well to recall that the white creole also took some time to establish himself in the new industry.

The reasons for this were many and again, perhaps, understandable in the context of the times. As we have seen, the pioneering oil companies found Trinidad in an undeveloped state.

The labour force, based purely on agriculture, was unskilled and it did in find a ready market for its services in the new industry. But it was quick to adapt to the new environment and skills required of it, and with training and experience developed an artisan class which gave a new dignity to labour undreamt of in the purely agricultural era.

The development of this artisan class, nurtured and stimulated by the oil companies' apprentice training schemes, is probably one of the major sociological benefits derived from our oil age. It opened-up horizons to which the labouring class could aspire and produced a new element in the society, the highly skilled craftsman and technician, who has played so significant a part in the industrialisation of the island during the past thirty years.

But while labour found a ready market for its services in the new industry and seized on the opportunity for advancement through the artisan class, the position was somewhat different for the middle and upper class. The industry needed professional and experienced personnel for its supervisory staff but these were unavailable locally. Thus the pattern of an expatriate staff with local labour was inevitable and it was to take some years for this pattern to be eroded. But this pattern was by no means unique to Trinidad today when compared with other underdeveloped countries of the emerging oil world. In 1930 oil there was not a single "National" on the staff of the international oil company with which I worked in Egypt, while in Rumania and the Argentine the percentage of "nationals" on our staff was negligible. The position with our neighbour Venezuela, at the birth of its oil industry and for many a long year, was similar as can be testified to by the hundreds of Trinidadians who reaped a rich harvest in Maracaibo. In Trinidad, the breakthrough of local personnel on to the staff of the oil companies probably preceded that of many other undeveloped countries.

By 1920 two or three of the pioneer companies were firmly established and could look to the future with some degree of confidence. They therefore decided to recruit and train young Trinidadians to replace the highly paid American drillers who dominated the industry and such young men were readily available from among those who had returned from the war. This was the first major breakthrough by local personnel to the staff of the oil companies. No sooner, however, had these young men completed their training and taken their places alongside their American counterparts than they became restless at not receiving the high salaries being paid to the Americans. They felt that they were being discriminated against and so when the Maracaibo boom developed in the mid 1920s, off they went in search of the new El Dorado.

Maracaibo proved to be a tremendous boost to the ego of the aspiring young Trinidadian in search of a career in oil. In Venezuela, he was accepted as an equal by his counterparts the British and American expatriates; he had learned his trade the hard way and on his return to Trinidad he was accepted as bearing the hallmark of international experience. And so, as always, the two sides of the coin emerged. The young Trinidadian considering himself discriminated against at home became the expatriate in Venezuela and reaped a rich harvest!

But while the Trinidadian gradually found a niche in the oil industry he was slow to grasp the full implications of the technological age which was unfolding. The industry needed, besides drillers, well-pullers, and refinery operators, professional engineers and scientists and these were unavailable locally. The Trinidadian, born into a traditional agricultural environment, had come to associate a profession with Law or Medicine. There was no tradition towards engineering and its related sciences as there was in the industrialised metropolitan countries, and it was not until the 1950s that he began to turn his thoughts towards a technological career. This is exemplified by the fact that when Trinidad Leaseholds Ltd. offered its first science scholarship at Mona in 1950 there were only four applicants. The eventual recipient of this scholarship —an employee of the Company — returned as a research chemist in 1953. Since that date, stimulated by the establishment of the University of the West Indies and the grant of scholarships by the oil companies and other industrial firms, there has been a steady and increasing output of local graduate engineers and technologists, but they were off to a late start. This is the reason why more Trinidadians have not yet reached the highest positions in our oil industry.

The oil industry has been criticised on this score but when it is realised that the local graduate engineer is the product of only the last ten, or at most twenty, years then the critics might think again. In the 1950s the Trinidadian graduates in the sciences could have been counted on the fingers of one hand; today Texaco employs hundreds spread over every sphere of its activities.

How many of us, I wonder, remember the days, not so very long ago, when the locomotives on our railway were manned by English drivers. The fathers of today's artisans, technicians and engineers were not considered as being capable of driving a locomotive! If this is a measure of the distance travelled in one generation, are there any limits to the heights to which we can aspire?

CROWD witness a well "flow in" at Guayaguayare in 1900.

OIL Installation in the twenties.

OIL WELL drilling. A derrick of the twenties.

THE author (centre) and his first company car – 1926.

CHAPTER XIII

THE POST WAR YEARS

WITH the end of the war and the return of the young men from overseas, the years 1919 and 1920 were gay and carefree. Each shipload of returning "heroes" rated a dance or reception of some sort in their honour and there were parties galore. Every planter now had his motor-car and the country districts were no longer isolated as they had been. The price of cocoa was good and there was the general feeling that the young men who had returned from the trenches were entitled to a good time before they settled down.

There were, however, no places of public entertainment; no cinemas, restaurants or night clubs and young people had to organize their own form of entertainment. This took the form of subscription dances in private homes, kindly lent by the owners with the occasional charity ball at the Princes Building or the Queen's Park Hotel. These dances were strictly formal affairs. The chaperoning of young ladies was still in vogue but was gradually being relaxed to the extent that they could be escorted to a dance by their brothers instead of being under the watchful eye of parents! But I can recall father's wrath and consternation at his daughter being invited to a dance without an invitation being issued to her parents: "What was the world coming to and who did the promoters of the dance think his daughter was!" In spite of the easing of strict chaperoning, however, the social circle remained rigid and a dance was a formal affair. Dance programmes were the order of the day, those little cards listing the tunes to be played, with their little pencils attached with pink or blue silk cord — and you were lucky, indeed, if you secured two or more dances for the evening with your girl of the moment. Indeed, to dance more than two or three dances with the same girl was likely to bring looks of disapproval and gossip from the chaperones. We danced the waltz, the foxtrot and the one-step — the days of the wiggles, the shakes and the jump-up were still many years away!

At the end of each dance, you escorted your partner into the garden where chairs were discreetly placed in twos and you sought those in the shadows. When the music re-started you escorted your partner back to the dance floor and handed her over to her chaperone.

Supper was invariably served at midnight and you picked your girl of the moment for the supper-dance which preceded it. Young ladies did not drink hard liquor and Coca Cola had not been heard of but there was always the bowl of sauterne, or you joined a group to share a bottle of champagne with your supper. "Formal and dull " will cry the youth of today, but we invariably danced till dawn.

Then there were the weekend picnics down the islands or the house parties at the estate houses in the country. The country house party and the hospitality of the planters have gone but what an institution they were. A house full of young people for the weekend, all going off to church on Sunday morning to return for rum punches and a table laden with souse and chicken; the young men boasting that they had done forty miles an hour in Dad's car in coming up the Valencia long stretch; father insisting that the young men wear a jacket to sit at lunch. Today I accept my young guests in their bathing trunks and their girlfriends in their bikinis and feel that the old man missed a lot. After lunch we would all gather sleepily on the gallery while someone wound up the Victrola to play the latest dance tunes.

Then there was the Christmas race meeting to climax the year's social whirl. The crowds and the fields were small by today's standards but the race meeting was a social event rather than a punter's delight. For the young man the event rated a new suit, with straw boater or Panama hat, while the girls turned out in Ascot fashion. The Police band played during the intervals, the Governor's Box was located in the middle of the grandstand and gentlemen doffed their hats as they walked by. I cannot recall whether "Tote" betting had yet been introduced in 1919 but in any case we were not interested in betting but organized our own shilling sweepstake among our group.

Apart from its dances and the races, Port of Spain had little to offer by way of amusement or entertainment. At sundown everyone took the air around the Pitch-Walk and here one went to meet one's friends. In the old days the ladies had been driven around the savannah in their carriages but now they did so in their open touring cars and the young men who were lucky enough to borrow Dad's car did likewise. The motor-car was sufficiently novel to enjoy driving and there was room on the roads on which to drive. The thing to do was to put down the top and cruise around the savannah in search of your girl friends who were out walking in groups and invite them for a drive. You then circled the savannah a few times or took the longer route round the Long Circular Road before dropping in at some hospitable home for a drink before dinner.

Carnival which had been suppressed during the war years was back with us in 1920 but it bore little resemblance to the lavish spectacle of today. It was still the wild and somewhat vulgar display of my boyhood days and was confined to downtown Port-of-Spain; few respectable citizens ventured south of Park Street. Masked costume balls had, however, been traditional with the French Creoles during the Carnival season and the highlight of the 1920 season was the costume ball at the Princes Building on Carnival Monday. At this ball, perhaps for the first time, the trend was towards organized bands rather than individual costumes. There were several such bands, twenty or thirty strong, and on the following Tuesday afternoon these bands paraded around the savannah on decorated lorries and threw streamers and confetti at the on-lookers. Out of this small beginning was to emerge the band competitions at the Country Club and other institutions which were the forerunners of today's spectacular band competitions. It was not until 1949, however, when the Trinidad Guardian organized its parade of bands in the savannah that the Carnival of today emerged with its movement to the up-town area and the mass participation of all classes. In the meantime the steelband was emerging and when the Carnival Development Committee took over its organisation in 1957, Carnival attained its full maturity as the Greatest Show on Earth, but I like to think that our drive around the savannah in 1920 was a milestone in the march of progress.

But Carnival 1920 was, perhaps, a fitting climax to our end of the war holiday. As the new year dawned most of the young men who had returned from the war began to drift into jobs — the lure of the new oil industry was calling many to far off Point Fortin and Fyzabad and it was also beckoning to me.

In my boyhood days in Manzanilla, before I went off to school in Ireland, those early oil pioneers John Cadman, Beeby Thompson and Cunningham Craig had been frequent visitors to our estate as they combed the island for signs of oil. I was enthralled by their tales of faraway lands and gushing oil wells and by their enthusiasm at the future prospects of oil in Trinidad and so at an early age I was bitten by the lure of oil. With the help of John Cadman I had been accepted at the University of Birmingham but my term was not to start until September and so to fill in time I got a job at Woodford Lodge Estate. I knew nothing of sugar and less about the handling of labour but Paul de Verteuil was manager of Woodford Lodge and he was my uncle and so at $40 per month I was a shift overseer in the factory. I shared a small house with two other overseers and worked a twelve-hour shift from six to six. The hours were long and exacting.

The grinding of the cane went on until 5 p.m. on Saturday but then the day shift carried on until all the juice had been safely boiled down, and this generally took till midnight. The day shift of that week then took up the night shift at 6 p.m. on Sunday for the following week. There was little time off, but there were beautiful horses on the estate and our Sunday morning recreation consisted of galloping along the cane traces to end up at neighbouring Waterloo for a drink with the overseers there.

The old factory at Woodford Lodge was on its last legs, spare parts had been unobtainable during the war years, but somehow it had been kept going and this was its last crop before a major overhaul. So each morning as Paul de Verteuil made his rounds at 5 a.m. there was a smile on his face as he learnt that the old mills had stood up for another 24 hours.

When the crop was over, I sailed off to England to start my career in oil but in spite of the passing years I am overcome with a sense of nostalgia at the smell of fermenting canes as today I drive through the cane belt in crop time.

CHAPTER XIV

THE OILFIELDS OF THE TWENTIES

WHEN I graduated from the University of Birmingham in 1923 the international oil industry was still in its infancy and was only just beginning to set its sights towards scientific development. There were some theories as to how petroleum had been formed and the most likely areas in which it might be found but the highly sophisticated technology of today was still a very long way off. Little was known of the chemistry of petroleum; the refinery process consisted merely of straight distillation yielding gasolene, kerosene and fuel oil; the myriads of by products which were to be developed through the petro-chemical industry were undreamt of while an oil well in excess of two thousand feet was a deep well!

John Cadman, later Baron Cadman, had been Professor of Mining at the University of Birmingham when he came to Trinidad to advise the colonial government on its future oil policy. As a mining engineer he recognized the need for a specialist engineer in the young and growing oil industry and established his school of petroleum as an adjunct to his Faculty of Mining at Birmingham. I was one of the early graduates of that school and the first Trinidadian graduate to enter the infant Trinidad oil industry.

When I arrived in Trinidad in August 1923 and informed my family that I had secured a job with the Kern Trinidad Oilfields at Guapo they were horrified. They had heard of La Brea and the Pitch Lake, but Guapo? Was that not a fever hole from which few white men returned alive? But the oil industry had already had its impact on Guapo and on the deep South; yellow fever had been eliminated and so I survived.

There on the beach at Guapo, soon after emancipation, William Burnley had landed his first shipment of freed American slaves to work his extensive sugar plantations in the area, but sugar cultivation had long been abandoned. Burnley's Perseverance Estate had passed to Conrad Stollmeyer and it was now a flourishing cocoa estate. However, as the oil fever developed around him Conrad Stollmeyer and his overseer had man-handled a second-hand percussion rig into the far end of his estate and there, at the depth of only 250 feet, had struck one of the most spectacular gushers in the early history of Trinidad's oil.

Beeby Thompson who was intimately associated with the early development of the area gives this account of the Stollmeyer venture in his delightful book, *Oil Pioneer*:

> "About this time (1912) an estate owner who had declined all our offers for his Perseverance Estate at Guapo known to have promising oil potentialities determined to drill himself where others had struck oil in the vicinity. In truly parsimonious fashion he had provided himself with a second-hand antiquated rig and entrusted its working to some unqualified but cheap operators who ferreted a well down somehow with quaint antedeluvian tools. At a depth of only 250 feet a rich oil sand was unexpectedly struck and such a violent and sustained outburst of heavy oil followed that the immediate vicinity became flooded with oil which ran into the nearby Vance river and out into the Gulf polluting everything along the river course and turning the sandy beach into a dreadful mess.
>
> "Unprovided with any means of control my colleague and representative C.E. Buch offered to shut in the well, but Stollmeyer declined assistance saying that he did not intend to interfere with the actions of nature consequently most of the oil was lost. On June 17th 1912 Buch had wired that the well had given about 80,000 barrels of oil and was flowing 500 barrels a day and when visited it was still giving periodical flows of some magnitude."

One can perhaps appreciate Beeby Thompson's pique at having been beaten out of this rich bonanza by the amateur Stollmeyer! Stollmeyer eventually came to terms with the Kern Group, and Perseverance Estate was now an established oil camp. The other camps in 1923 were Tabaquite, Forest Reserve, Apex, Point Fortin and Barrackpore, while the Pitch Lake Camp at Brighton had predated them all. The Brighton camp had been established to exploit the Pitch Lake but had been expanded when the Asphalt Company joined the oil producing ranks. There was also Pointe-a-Pierre, with its small refinery, nestling under Pointe-a-Pierre Hill in the small area between the southern Main Road and the sea.

The Kern Camp consisted of seven married staff bungalows and the bachelors' mess where I joined a motley group of English and Scots engineers and American drillers. My salary was $125 per month but our mess bill was only $25 and income tax was sixpence in the pound! Our quarters consisted of two rows of rooms, back to back, surrounded by an eight foot wide mosquito screened gallery which was our recreation area. Across the paved yard was the Mess Hall. By some process of natural segregation the inmates had grouped themselves into four clubs and staked their claims to one of the four corners of the gallery where they gathered each evening around their bottle of rum. I was accepted into the north-west corner by the younger group. The American drillers held another corner while a third corner was occupied by Frank and Bill. These two young Englishmen had discovered our rum cocktail soon after their arrival in Trinidad and each evening at five o'clock the house boy placed a bowl of ice, a jug and swizzle stick on their small table and Frank and Bill sat and swizzled! Bill was a somewhat plump and pink young man who had arrived in Trinidad complete with tails and opera hat and no doubt missed his evening stroll through London's Piccadilly Circus. When nostalgia and rum cocktails combined the effect on Bill was startling. He would strip to his birthday suit, don only his tails and opera hat and stroll around the gallery doffing his hat to imaginary girlfriends, looking for all the world like a pink cherub. Years later I was to read of Bill's promotion to the top executive position of a Middle East oil company and I wondered whether he presided over his Board meetings with the same flair that he had exhibited on our Kern gallery.

Just outside of the main camp and approximately set on the top of a hill stood number seven bungalow where John Stokes, the General Manager, resided. John Stokes had risen from the ranks through drilling oil wells all over California and there was little that he did not know of his trade. He was fascinated by the excitement of the early oil industry and as he once confided to me, "I just love to see 'em flow". This was when we had a wild gusher on our hands. On such occasions, and they were frequent, he would stand under his large umbrella for hours, always with one eye on the flow, as he turned to any bystander with the query "What do you think she's making?" and the larger the estimate he got the more pleased he was.

Today's highly efficient organisation of the industry which makes it necessary for every member of the field staff to be provided with some form of motor transport did not apply to Kern in the early twenties. The General Manager had a car and the Drilling Superintendent a pick-up, but the rest of us walked or depended on a passing truck to get around the field. John Stokes was, however, always prepared to give one a lift with one proviso. His Buick was a gleaming treasure and had to be kept spotless for Mrs. Stokes, so when John offered a lift he would enquire, "Is your siddown clean?" and if your pants were oily, as they usually were, you did not enter the Buick but you hung on to the running board!

My arrival at Kern coincided with the establishment by Government of the newly created Petroleum Department with offices in San Fernando. The department was headed by a young American Petroleum Engineer, Fred Zeigler, and G.A.P. Southwell who had graduated from Birmingham two years ahead of me. The new Department was starting from scratch to collect the data on all wells so far drilled on the island and my first assignment was to assemble and collate the Kern data for its files. This entailed the reading of reams of daily drilling reports written in the picturesque jargon of the early American drillers, a truly fascinating insight into lucid reporting. The notation, "She's off to the races" I was advised, could only mean that the well in question had blown out! But my assignment was eventually completed and my histories of the early Kern wells are today no doubt buried somewhere in our Petroleum archives!

I then became a sort of Jack-of-all-trades. John Stokes was somewhat vague as to where a university graduate fitted with his organisation and I was free to roam the field and learn the intricacies of the oil game. I was Geologist when I spent hours collecting cuttings from the well as the drill neared the depth at which I had hopefully predicted an oil sand and thrilled at that first smell of oil which heralded success. I was Chemist when I sampled a tank and took it to the refinery at Point Fortin for analysis. I was Civil Engineer when I surveyed the route for a new road or pipeline through the forest. I was Lease Hound when the Chinese shopkeeper in the village suggested that my credit might be enhanced if I would persuade the company to lease his friend's ten acre parcel. There was lots to learn of the oil industry in the early twenties!

The luxury of the eight-hour day and the forty-hour week had not been dreamt of. Drilling operations were carried out on the basis of two twelve-hour shifts seven days a week, holidays included, and as all the services on the field were geared to keep the drilling rigs going, everyone was "on call' twenty-four hours a day. But we kept our fingers crossed and prayed that no crisis would develop as we sneaked off to a dance at a neighbouring club or a weekend in Port of Spain.

Kern being a relatively new and small camp did not have a clubhouse nor recreational facilities for its staff, as did the large camps, but these were available to us at Point Fortin and Brighton where we were always made welcome. The difficulty, however, was getting there as no one on our staff owned a car although it sometimes possible, on special occasions, to borrow the one company service car. This was not good enough for me so I invested in my first car. This was a somewhat ancient Ford two-seater for which I paid $45 and it actually ran. It took a great deal of cranking to get it started but once started it could get me to Port of Spain in three hours if the tyres held out. These were the days before detachable rims or spare wheels, a puncture or blowout, and these were frequent, meant taking off the tyre, affixing a patch to the tube and pumping up the tyre with a hand-pump.

The drive to and from Port of Spain was always an adventure. With the windshield raised and the hood down it was an exhilarating experience to leave Port of Spain at 4 a.m. in the hope of being in camp before the 7 o'clock whistle. The old car seemed to purr in the cool of the morning and as you crested Pointe-a-Pierre hill as dawn was breaking, you knew you were doing well and would have time for an acra and float from the old lady under the shop gallery in San Fernando. What has happened to the all-night acra and float stand? Alas! It has been replaced by the roti parlour. Is this because the East Indian entrepreneur has outstripped the Negro? Or, is it because in our sophistication we have turned from salt-fish to chicken and shrimp?

There was little traffic on the road in the early morning as one left Port of Spain except for the occasional line of donkey carts piled high with bags of charcoal for the morning market. Lit by a dim flambeau, with the drivers asleep on their sacks of coal, they were a greater menace on the road than today's taxis. There was the occasion, however, on which some motorists got their own back on the charcoal carts. Leaving town after a dance, a party of my young friends encountered a charcoal train. They stopped and quietly turned all the donkeys homeward and set them on their way while their owners slept. The train headed back into the country, history does not record how far, but the market was short of charcoal that morning.

As I owned a car, my brothers, one at Brighton and the other at Point Fortin, depended on me for their transportation when there was a dance or party at one of the camps. There was, however, the problem of communication as the telephone could not always be relied upon but it did work in our favour on one memorable occasion. I had called brother at Point Fortin at the same moment brother at Brighton had called him, and, with all the lines nicely crossed in our favour, we got involved in a three-way conversation trying to discover who had called whom and for what. Then a fourth very angry voice cut in. "It's no bloody good, Mac, all the damn O'Connors are on the line."

But while telephone communication was problematical, the new medium, radio, was dawning and there were those enthusiasts who boasted that they had heard New York or Denver on shortwave sets. One such was John Moodie, the Managing Director of Tennants Estates. The marvels of this new were explained to us one morning as a group of workmen sheltered from the rain in a field boiler shed. Ah tell you, man," explained our informant, "Mr. Moodie does have dis ting call radio and if something happen in New York, Mr. Moodie does know befo' it happen."

Apart from work, our main preoccupation was soccer but our league of the twenties was strictly confined to the staff clubs. While cricket had been our national game for many a year and was played in remotest villages where any bare-footed boy could fashion a bat from a piece of boxwood and raid the nearest orange tree for balls, soccer had not reached the masses, who in any case had no facilities for the game. In the oil areas the only playing fields were those attached to the senior staff Clubs at Brighton, Point Fortin, Forest Reserve and Pointe-a-Pierre and soccer was therefore a white man's game. We had our stars in Hugh Thom of Brighton and Davy Law of Point Fortin but our overall standard could not have been very high as I sometimes got a pick for Point Fortin! Our League was, however, keenly contested, but Pointe-a-Pierre usually headed the league table and the reason was not hard to find for their sponsor and coach was none other than Hugh MacCrea! Like all true Scots, Mac was a soccer enthusiast, and, as Manager of the Pointe-a-Pierre stores, it was generally accepted that only the soccer stars of Queen's Royal College and St. Mary's College had any chance of a position on his staff! But Mac was not only a soccer enthusiast, he was a man of many parts and the stories of his wit and pranks were legion and are still repeated when oldtimers of the industry meet today. My favourite: as Stores Superintendent, Mac was also in charge of the Company's grocery, when an irate housewife phoned him. "Mr. Mac, my milk has all gone sour." "Lady" advised Mac, "you better call your doctor! "

But to return to soccer, the highlight of the season was our annual North-South match when we invited one of the white Port of Spain Clubs — Shamrock or Casuals — down for the weekend. They came supported by their girlfriends and the match was followed by a grand ball at Willie Colley's Paramount Hotel in San Fernando.

In addition to soccer we also had our inter-oilfield athletic meetings. Organized for the first time in 1927 this annual event ran for several years and like soccer was confined to members of the staff club. In the twenties we had not yet learnt of the levelling influence of sport.

Apart from soccer and the annual sports meeting the social life in the oil camps revolved around the clubhouse and the tennis courts, bridge and the small dinner party. With the exception of the formal annual dance at the three or four larger camps there were few large gatherings. The cocktail party of today was unheard of, the main means of entertaining being the dinner party of eight or twelve, and if one did not play bridge one was a social outcast for a dinner party meant a rubber or two before dinner followed by more bridge over coffee and liqueurs.

But while we in the camps enjoyed our social round and worked in relatively comfortable surroundings, the conditions in the neighbouring villages were poor and squalid. The oil companies had as yet made no effort to house their labour force and as the fields grew and attracted more and more labour the adjacent villages were bursting at the seams and there was an acute shortage of housing. There were no social amenities in these villages, no recreational facilities other than the rum shops and no public transport. Few workmen could afford a bicycle and a worker, after his twelve hour shift, might have to walk four or six miles to get home. There was the occasional "bus" linking the outlying villages with San Fernando. These, converted one-ton Ford trucks, with wooden seats nailed to the deck and a brightly coloured canvas canopy had such picturesque names as the "La Brea Belle" and the "Cedros Bee" emblazoned on their sides but their schedule was unpredictable and their arrival at destination problematical.

Indeed, the oilfields of the twenties presented a very different picture from those of today. There were no gleaming silver tanks and towering steel derricks, no glittering gathering stations and well-ordered lanes of pipelines snaking through the forest. The transition from Cable Tool drilling to the Rotary method was still in progress. The Combination System was generally installed at every drilling site and the Cable Tool end with its squat wooden derrick was left in place on the completion of drilling to service the well in its production stages. We did not wear safety hats or safety boots; in any case the labour force was mostly barefooted. Today's emphasis on "good housekeeping" and "safety" would have been considered sissy talk. The job on hand was "to drill 'em and let 'em flow" into the large pits which surrounded the well site. There was heavy black oil everywhere and the efficiency of the field staff was judged by the amount of oil on one's clothing!

There were few labour saving devices. Heavy equipment was headed into place by man power, the forests were cleared by the axe-man, and well sites and roads were graded by that unique breed of men and their women folk, the "Tattoo Gang". Earth work was paid for by the cubic yard dug and moved and the "Tattoo Gang" could move mountains. The men dug the wet earth with fork and shovel and piled the wooden trays high for their women partner to head it to the "fill" in an endless procession to and from like a swarm of bachacs. The bulldozer has replaced the "Tattoo Gang" but the miles of road through our forests remain as a silent monument to a very special breed of men and their women folk who have passed into oblivion.

But the twenties were to end on a note of tragedy with the most spectacular and disastrous fire in Trinidad's oil history. The story of the Dome Fire started with the obstinacy of an old East Indian land owner. He owned a ten-acre block in the middle of the rich Apex field at Fyzabad. He had once had a dispute with the Company and although the Company had successfully drilled all around him, he had stubbornly refused to lease his land to them. Eventually, a small local company was formed to drill the area and a young Trinidad driller was persuaded to undertake the drilling for a share in the venture. Bob Wade had been a boyhood friend of ours, having been brought up on a neighbouring estate at Sangre Grande. He somehow assembled a drilling rig to drill the first well. All went well; the well was successfully completed and "came in" with a large flow. Everything seemed to be well under control and Bob Wade left for the Country Club to celebrate his good fortune. As darkness fell, however, a small leak developed in one of the control valves and within hours the well was out of control, spouting oil and gas into the air. The whole surrounding area was covered with oil and the air saturated with gas. The owner and his entire family rushed to the scene, rejoicing no doubt in the thought that they had struck it rich. Bob Wade hurried back from Port of Spain in an attempt to cap the well when the whole area exploded. What remained of Bob Wade was found in his car. He had apparently tried to start his engine so as to focus his headlights on the well head and this had sparked the holocaust. The whole Indian family perished and several workmen.

The Dome Field was later successfully exploited and was reported to be one of the richest ten-acre blocks ever drilled in Trinidad, but the sequel to the Dome Venture was as tragic as its beginning. The sole heir to the property was a youngster by the name of Partap. He built himself a mansion in the village of St. Mary's, Oropouche, where surrounded by a high wall he lived as a hermit. Years later he was murdered in his home and his murder has remained an unsolved mystery.

The Dome tragedy shook us all in the oil belt. There had been so many occasions, experienced by us all, when the ingredients for similar holocausts had been ever present during the "gusher period". As we neared the end of the twenties, however, there were signs of impending change. At Kern, John Stokes had left us and his place as General Manager had been taken by an English geologist. Perhaps, this was symptomatic of the change. The oil industry was coming of age and moving into the era of the technologist. The American oil journals were full of new and exciting techniques being tried out throughout the world and Trinidad was moving with the times. One of these new discoveries was that by weighting the drilling fluid used in rotary drilling with barytes (barium sulphate) the high pressures encountered while drilling through the oil horizons could be controlled. Tests had proved successful and United British Oilfields of Trinidad brought in a complete drilling crew from California to introduce the method into Trinidad. Their first experiment ended in tragedy, however, as in spite of the heavy fluid the well did blow and caught fire resulting in the loss of several lives. The tests were, however, continued, and thus was born a new science, the technology of drilling fluids which was to revolutionise the drilling industry and make possible the fantastic depths achieved today.

These developments were just being started in Trinidad in 1929 when my second three-year contract with Kern came to an end. The outside world looked exciting and I sailed for England in August in search of new horizons.

CHAPTER XV

1937

AFTER an absence of eight years during which I had worked on the oilfields of Rumania, Egypt and Argentina with a year at the head office of Shell in the Hague I returned home, perhaps appropriately on Discovery Day 1937, to re-discover a new and rapidly changing Trinidad. The main topic of conversation on my arrival was, of course, the oilfields' riots of the previous June but few of us then realised that the events of 1937 were to herald in a new era in so many facets of our lives.

The riots had been sparked when the police attempted to arrest Tubal Uriah Butler as he was addressing a mass meeting in Fyzabad on the evening of June 19. Butler was born in Grenada; he had seen service abroad with the West India Regiment during World War I, and had then come to Trinidad like so many of his countrymen, lured by prospects of employment in the oil industry. The story was that he had been injured on the job, which had left him with a permanent limp, for which he had failed to receive any compensation. This had embittered him against his employers. Be that as it may he had set himself up as the champion of the labouring class and formed a political-cum-labour organisation under the high-sounding name of the "British Empire Workers and Citizens Home Rule Party" and proclaimed himself to be the "Chief Servant" of the people. He had his own particular flair for oratory and showmanship, a mixture of religious fervour and anger against social injustice which quickly won him a large following in the oil belt. His speeches were violent and some of his utterances may have been seditious.

The authorities considered him a trouble-maker and a warrant was issued for his arrest. But by one of the most glaring instances of ineptitude and lack of commonsense the police attempted to serve the warrant as he was addressing a public meeting! It was tantamount to throwing the proverbial match into the keg of gunpowder. The crowd rushed the police and firing broke out. The Police Inspector leading the arrest was shot dead and Butler escaped into the crowd. But he was pursued by a corporal who in turn was chased by the crowd, caught, beaten and burnt to death by the angry mob. Within hours the oilfields were paralysed by a general strike which quickly spread to the sugar estates and to the municipal workers of San Fernando. Gathering momentum, the oil workers marched through the town, causing all shops and business places to close. On the oilfields, members of the staff were confined to their camps. The men were sworn in as Special Constables and issued with arms while those women who could hurried into Port of Spain.

It was not until June 22 when Royal Marines were landed from the cruisers Ajax and Exeter that some semblance of order began to be established and it was the first week in July before the strike was officially over. The difficulty throughout the disturbances, facing both Government and the employers was that there were no leaders of the workers with whom they could deal. Butler had gone into hiding with a reward of $500 offered for information as to his whereabouts and there was no one to take his place.

Eventually talks were opened between various groups. The Borough Council of San Fernando met its workers and granted wage increases ranging from 5 to 15 cents per day, the maximum wage of a labourer being brought up to 75 cents per day. Wage increases were granted by the Usine St. Madeleine sugar factory and an arbitration board finally awarded an increase of 3 cents per hour to the oil workers.

The Royal Commission which subsequently investigated the causes of the riot was outspoken on the evils of the day: the deplorable housing conditions of the labouring classes and the entire absence of any form of industrial relations machinery through which the working class could air their grievances. There is no need to describe again the humiliating. conditions of the villages which had sprung up in the oil belt. There had been apparently no improvement during my absence, rather, conditions seemed to have worsened. The Royal Commission reported:

"If housing of workers residing in agricultural estates leaves much to be desired, the conditions in some of the villages are even more unsatisfactory. An example of this is to be seen in the case of Fyzabad, a village which has grown up on the edge of the oilfields without any apparent regulation or control or observance of elementary rules as to structure, space or sanitation and which forms a suitable rendezvous for all the undesirable elements which congregate in the neighbourhood of new industrial developments where men obtaining comparatively high wages are to be found. In the recent disturbances Fyzabad was the centre of activity of the hooligan element which played so conspicuous a part in the attempts to provoke riot and damage to life and property. Similar examples of the worst village housing conditions adjacent to the oilfield exist at Frisco Junction, Point Fortin and Cochran Village Guapo."

As to the lack of any form of industrial machinery the Commission had this to say:

"Had there existed in the oilfields and elsewhere organised means of collective bargaining through which claims of the work people could have found ample means of expression there can be little doubt that the disturbances which subsequently occurred might have been avoided."

While it was to take some years before the slum areas of Fyzabad and Point Fortin could be the villages of today, and the war years were to intervene, the impact of the riots on the labour scene was immediate. Butler emerged as the hero of the "uprising" but he had neither the temperament nor the ability to organise a Trade Union and it therefore fell to John Rojas and Ralph Mentor to do so with the formation of the Oilfields Workers Trade Union which has over the years revolutionised the status of the oil worker and set the pattern for industrial relations throughout the islands.

The year 1937 also marked a turning point in political history of the island. The Royal Commission noted the widespread and growing political consciousness among the masses which had been awakened by Cipriani and which it felt could not be ignored. The people wanted a say in their affairs but they were disenfranchised. The Commission recommended a reduction in the number of nominated members to the Legislature and an increase in elected membership while at the same time it proposed a broadening of the voters' qualifications. The seeds of political emancipation were sown, but the war clouds were gathering over Europe and it was 1946 before the first elections were held under full adult franchise and the march towards nationhood could get under way.

While the strikes and riots of 1937 were the most dramatic happening during my absence abroad other significant events had also taken place which heralded the new era into which we were entering. Pan American Airlines had established its sea plane base at Cocorite and was flying a regular service to Miami — thus Trinidad had entered the air transport age. The deep water harbour was nearing completion and the imposing new Treasury Building was rising on Marine (now Independence) Square. The "cabby" and his horse drawn cab had given way to the taxi and "one-way" traffic had been established on Frederick Street but the trams still ran. On the entertainment and social scene the Country Club had been opened, the silent films had given way to the "talkies" and Pierre Sands presided over his French restaurant in St. Anns.

On the industrial scene, sugar production had doubled and oil production had grown from 5 million to 13 million barrels per year. The Penal field had been discovered and Trinidad Petroleum Development Company had established its Beach Camp at Palo Seco. The cocoa industry on the other hand had been ruined by the Witch's Broom disease and low prices and with its demise had ended a way of life in the country districts. The days of the French Creole plantocracy were over; few of the old families remained in the once prosperous Manzanilla and Montserrat areas and gone were the weekend house parties of the twenties.

The oil company to which I returned was new to Trinidad. The Antilles Petroleum Co., a subsidiary of McColl Frontenac of

Canada had been formed to take over the oil leases of the Asphalt Company surrounding the Pitch Lake and was busy acquiring acreage through the island. Its staff camp overlooking Vessigny Bay just south of Brighton was under construction and I had to leave my wife in Port of Spain while I took up residence in the Bachelors' Mess at Brighton until a bungalow was ready for us. Brighton, full of memories of the past, when it had been the social centre of oilfield life, had not changed. All the old faces were still there to welcome me back.

When we did, a month later, move into our new bungalow at the Antilles Camp it was to find many innovations undreamt of in the old days. A refrigerator replaced the ice-box, hot and cold flowed in the tiled bath-room, a gas cooker took the place of the smoky wood fire stove in the kitchen. The amenities of modern living had come to the oil belt. It was, however, on the operating of the oilfields that the greatest revolution had taken place. Trinidad oil industry had come of age and all the new and remarkable developments which I had seen taking place during my time abroad had been introduced. The advent of electrical logging and the gun perforator had revolutionised well completion methods, the development of the blow-out preventer and heavy drilling made the spectacular gushers of the twenties a thing of the past. Gone were the days when "we drilled 'em and let 'em flow". Science and technology were replacing the rough and ready methods of the pioneers.

But while a good deal of material progress had been made, there was little evidence of change in the social structure. The disturbances of 1937 had dramatised the conditions of the working class but the Colonial Government and the "Society" remained established on the old three-tiered strata with its distinctive bands. True there was, as there had always been, a slight diffusion of the colours at the contact planes but the striations clear cut and unmistakable. All Government departments were headed by expatriate officers of the British Colonial Service and there were few, if any, coloured faces to be seen in the senior ranks of the local civil service. The County Wardens were exclusively drawn from the white element in the community and so were the commissioned officers of the Police

Force. The pattern was no different in industry and commerce. True, there were only three banks in Port of Spain, each with its branch in San Fernando, but a career in banking was reserved for the whites with the emphasis on the expatriate in the higher position. The oil industry had, from its inception, accepted the status quo and had seen no reason to rock the boat which had sailed so calmly for over a hundred years under the tri-colour standard. And so, as we passed from 1937, we hardly noticed the change of wind engendered by Cipriani and Butler and fanned by the growing political and social consciousness which was to bring about such radical changes in our society. But then the clouds of war were gathering around us and our little flurries were soon to be forgotten as we braced ourselves for the impending storm.

As we moved into 1939, I witnessed my first Carnival in Port of Spain for many a year. My wife had gone to Argentina to visit her family so I took my local leave to coincide with Carnival; but Carnival was still geared to its original concept and had not yet emerged into the spectacle of today. The bands on the streets were small by today's standard and the steelband had not yet emerged. I was told that the "in thing" to do was to join the young men who gathered at the bar of the Hotel de Paris and listen to the calypsonians who drifted in while we drank too many rum punches. There was no Carnival organisation and no parade of bands. For us, however, the highlight of Carnival was the band competition at the Country Club and I recall Conrad O'Brien's prize winning band of red-coated huntsmen complete with two live fox-hounds. There was to be no more carnival for several years but the stage had been set for the spectacular bands of the post-war era.

My other memory of that 1939 Carnival week was the inauguration of the Piarco Airport. K.L.M. had started a regular air service between Trinidad and Curacao and their pilots who were based on Port of Spain were the heroes of the girls in my young sisters' set. When, therefore, it was decided to officially inaugurate the air service, my sisters were among those invited to the ceremony at Piarco and being in town with a car I crashed the party as their escort. The "airfield" consisted of a short grass-grown runway with a small corrugated iron shed as booking office and waiting room. The girls were taken for a short flight over the field and we were served with a few drinks. That was the birth of Piarco International Airport. I do not believe that any of us on that quiet Sunday morning considered that within months it was to become a hive of activity as, with the outbreak of war, the Americans would move in and the British Fleet Air Arm would establish a training school there.

It was in 1939, too, that I had my first birds-eye view of Trinidad. A party of our company directors paid us a visit from Canada and thought it would be a good idea to see our operations from the air. A Pan-Am flying boat was chartered for the afternoon and we took off from Cocorite into a cloudless sky to fly out over Point Fortin, Forest Reserve and out to Guayaguayare. It was I believe the first aerial survey of Trinidad!

CHAPTER XVI

THE WAR YEARS (AND AFTER)

WITHIN a few weeks of its outbreak the horrors and the realities of war were brought home to us by the sinking of the Simon Bolivar. The Bolivar was the pride of the Royal Netherlands Steam Ship Company which ran a regular service between Rotterdam and the Caribbean. Those of us on the oilfields knew her well as she regularly overnighted at Brighton and we were always made welcome on board for a drink of cold Dutch beer. It was a fine Sunday morning and we were on the beach at Brighton for our regular swim when the news broke. The morning papers had not yet reached us but someone picked up a news flash on the B.B.C. The Bolivar had struck one of Hitler's first magnetic mines in the North Sea and gone down. Her passengers were all West Indians who had taken this their first opportunity to cut short their holiday and hurry home on the outbreak of war. Most of us on the beach that morning had friends or relatives on board and we spent an anxious day waiting for news of the survivors. Luckily the loss was not as great as might have been expected but many a Trinidadian mourned the loss of a dear one.

Hitler had started his ruthless war at sea and it was this aspect of the war which was to have perhaps the greatest impact on Trinidad. Soon we were to follow the news of the first naval engagement of the war with special interest for it was the cruisers Exeter and Ajax, whose marines had landed in Trinidad in 1937 during the time of the oilfields' riots, which fought and won the epic battle of the River Plate. This brought back memories of the First World War in which Trinidad had also figured in the first naval engagement. On the outbreak of war in 1914, a unit of the West Indian fleet, the Good Hope, called at Port of Spain to pick up one of our prominent young surgeons, Fernand de Verteuil, who was on the naval reserve list. She then sailed for the South Atlantic and was sunk in the first naval engagement of the war. Dr. de Verteuil became the first Trinidad casualty of World War I and by a curious coincidence his aunt, Mrs. St. Yves de Verteuil, was among those lost on the Simon Bolivar. Thus the first Trinidad casualty in both World Wars was a member of one of our most prominent families. Throughout 1940 we sat glued to our radios each morning as Hitler overran Europe and we listened in awe and almost panic at the news of the epic withdrawal from Dunkirk. At this distance we could not conceive that Britain might be invaded and so we began to take hope as we listened to Winston Churchill's fighting speeches and as the Royal Air Force fought back to win the Battle of Britain.

It was in 1941, however, that Trinidad really got into the act of war with the signing of the Bases Agreement. England was fighting with her back against the wall. German submarines were taking a heavy toll of her shipping and American aid was vital to her survival. Under the Bases Agreement, Churchill got 50 old American destroyers, "mothballed" since World War I, from President Franklin Delano Roosevelt in exchange for the rights to establish American naval and army bases in the Caribbean. Trinidad's contribution was the Naval Base at Chaguaramas and the Army Base at Waller Field. The agreement was signed in March and overnight Trinidad became a hive of industry as the construction crews moved in followed by the army. Heavy transport cluttered our inadequate roads, rum and coca-cola flowed and, as immortalised by our calypsonians, "everyone was working for the Yankee Dollar!"

On the oilfields we became short of labour as the workers rushed for employment on the construction sites where, it was said, anyone who could lay his hands on a hammer or a saw was considered a skilled craftsman. But Trinidad oil was a vital necessity for the war effort and, short of labour or not, we had to carry on. Soon, too, we were short of steel and other essential equipment; these were needed for the armament industries and even when procurable they had to run the gauntlet of the submarine war to get to us. But oil was needed; priorities had to be established and so we came under the control of various Boards and Committees. One of these was set up by the oil industry itself to vet each company's drilling programme to ensure that the expected yield from every well drilled would justify the tonnage of steel used. The Trinidad oil industry was thus fully geared to the war effort and it played a not insignificant part in fuelling of the allied fleets and air forces.

In his "*Story of our Oil*" published in the Independence Supplement of the *Trinidad Guardian* in August 1971, Dr. Vernon Mulchansingh wrote:

> "In 1940 — 1941 what amounted to a new refinery was constructed by an American firm for the British Ministry Of Aircraft Construction (at Pointe-a-Pierre) to produce aviation fuel for the Royal Air Force and the U.S. Air Force. So important was the supply of products from Trinidad some years after the war the *Petroleum Times* commented that no Company in the world, certainly no British company, did so much for the war effort in relation to its size, as Trinidad Leaseholds Ltd".

Besides the shortage of steel and machinery on the oilfields the general public also soon began to feel the shortages of most consumer items — one of the most serious shortages being rubber. To conserve car and truck tyres all vehicles were zoned to their areas of operation and carried a large "P" for St. Patrick or "V" for Victoria painted on the bonnet. Thus Port of Spain became virtually out of bounds for most of us. We drank rum instead of whiskey, meat was often in short supply and we learnt to substitute green banana chips for potato chips at our cocktail parties.

The importance of our oil industry was supposed to make us vulnerable to enemy raids. There was, perhaps, the possibility that an enemy submarine could lob a few shells into Pointe-a-Pierre, or that a raiding party might attempt to blow up a tank so we had our Home Guard and our air-raid shelters. Every oil company had its platoon or company of the Home Guard depending on its size. Whether or not we could have held an enemy at bay is highly problematical but we took ourselves very seriously as we were instructed in the art of jungle warfare on Sunday mornings and learnt to dismantle and reassemble the odd Sten gun which was placed at our disposal. We had mock raids on each other's oil installations which generally ended up with the capture of the club house, for these raids were a thirsty business. There was the occasion on which we set out to attack Forest Reserve. We borrowed one of our company's trucks to transport our platoon to a suitable point from which we would organize our attack, but Reserve Camp cheated on us. They staged an ambush outside their camp and as we drove peacefully along we were greeted by a hail of blank rifle fire from the bushes. The driver of our truck, not a member of the Home Guard, of course, was so terrified that he promptly ran his truck into the ditch and the exercise was over.

As air raid warden for our camp it was one of my duties, on the sound of the alarm, to muster all the women and children and take care of them. We had periodic practice alarms during which we gathered at a suitable bungalow for coffee and cake. We did not take these alarms very seriously until one memorable morning when we were jolted out of our complacency. We had gathered as usual for our coffee party on the sound of an alarm when suddenly there a *Boom!* It sounded awfully like a distant explosion. There was a lull in the conversation, then a second *Boom!.* Was this the real thing? I strolled to the window, I hoped calmly, and there it was. We were building an air raid shelter, a large hole had been dug and workmen were covering it over with some old tank sheets. Instead of carrying these, however, the men were upending them and letting them fall forward. This was the Boom. With a sheepish grin, I returned to reassure my flock.

But we did have the real thing one night when a German sub. sneaked in through the Bocas and sank two ships anchored at Port of Spain. This was followed all night by terrific activity as planes flew over the Gulf dropping flares in a vain attempt to spot the sub. We never heard how the submarine had managed to elude the defences of the Bocas and escape unharmed.

Apart from our Home Guard and air-raid activities and at times acute shortages of certain items of food and everyday necessities, there was little disruption in our way of life. Most of our social gatherings were geared to some form of fund-raising for the war charities. The women attended First Aid classes and busied themselves making swabs and bandages for the Red

Cross. We learnt to play baseball with the American unit which was established at Green Hill in Cedros. And so the long years of the war went by, but the face of Trinidad had begun to change.

There are those among us who have severely criticized the Bases but in retrospect did we really do so badly out of the Invasion? During their relatively short stay (they did not all sit out their 99 years), they did not seriously disrupt our way of life and they certainly left us with many lasting amenities. They cleared thousands of acres in the Waller Field area and laid a network of roads all ready for our dairy and pig farmers. They built us the Churchill-Roosevelt Highway, at the time the first highway on the island; they gave us the scenic drive to Maracas; they opened up the Chaguaramas area and then handed it back with all its amenities; they extended the docking facilities at Port of Spain and gave lucrative employment to thousands of our people. All this when they were here and when we finally negotiated departure we extracted a few more millions of dollars as compensation which have gone into the J.F. Kennedy Complex at the Western Main Road and warehouses at the docks. Future historians will record that we came out on the credit side and if we can judge by the humorous portrayal of the American by our numerous sailor bands at Carnival it would not appear that the man in the street bore them any ill will.

To those of us who remember the war years as just part of our yesterdays it is often difficult to realise that over 67 per cent of present population was then unborn. This explains, perhaps, what we are pleased to call today the Generation Gap, for we live in an entirely new world. The younger generation tell us that they are dissatisfied at the rate of progress, they want change now for now, but not having experienced a yesterday how can they appreciate the dramatic overnight changes which have taken place in our political, economic and social environments?

When the Moyne Commission, which investigated the 1937 disturbances, recommended that "consideration be given to the broadening of the franchise" could they in their wildest dreams have foreseen the rapid march of political emancipation leading to nationhood within a quarter of a century? The advent of political emancipation set off a chain reaction in our economic and social environment which has been spectacular in its achievement and undreamt of by those of us of the pre-war generation.

With the new dawn has come the growth of the Trade Union movement and a tremendous rise in the standard of living of the working class, and, indeed, of all classes. Improved housing conditions — gone are the barrack rooms and tapia huts of the rural areas — have been accompanied by the extension of electricity and pipe-borne water supplies to the remotest areas, while secondary education is within reach of thousands instead of to the privileged few. We have our own University. The steel band has emerged from the back yards of Laventille to play in Madison Square Gardens and Carnival with its origin in Canboulay has become the Greatest Show on Earth.

Overnight, too, we have staged an industrial revolution which places Trinidad in the forefront of the developing countries of the world. The Trinidad of today is very different to that of our yesterdays.

But, perhaps, one of the most fundamental changes is that which has occurred in our social structure. We have dug into the foundations of that structure as it was laid down by our founding fathers, and seen how, in the context of times, it inevitably resulted in a community "the significant character of which" as noted by Wooding "was that it was divided pigmentally as well as economically, the less the pigmentation the more they dominated the scene - governmentally, economically, educationally and socially and indeed in every other way".

This "characteristic" underwent very little fundamental change during the colonial era with its concept of European supremacy and it was not until the last thirty years that a new social order evolved in which colour consciousness has been almost, if not entirely, eradicated and the racial barriers of yesterday forgotten.

It is the fashion of West Indian historians and politicians to blame all our ills, whether real or imaginary, on Colonialism, and especially on its epochs of slavery and indentured labour but none have ventured to speculate on how else the nations of the Caribbean could or would have evolved. Although we revere

Columbus and Discovery Day, it sometimes seems to be forgotten that Columbus was a European and that it was the Europeans who established the New World from Canada to Cape Horn. In the tropical areas of the Caribbean, however, the Europeans could not stand up to the rigours of manual labour in the sugar and cotton fields and so turned to Africa and then to India for the labour force. The conditions under which that labour force was introduced were harsh and inhuman but would the Africans and the East Indians have crossed the Atlantic to the New World under any other circumstances? As Trinidadians, therefore, we owe our existence to our Founding Fathers who brought us all here from the four corners of the earth. Our origins have been diverse and so, too, the conditions under which we arrived but in the final analysis a whole has been welded and a Nation has evolved. I feel frankly that in this Nation the majority of our citizens have attained a standard of living and social development that is far in advance of what they would have achieved in the countries of their origin and I am confident that our representatives, made up of our diverse races, today sit as equals with other leaders of the World in the Parliament of Nations.

APPENDIX

REPORT BY DR. J.L. O'CONNOR ON VISIT TO ESTATES AT CHAGUANAS
DATED 25th JULY, 1827.

ON Saturday the 21st July, 1827, I proceeded from town to the quarter Chaguanas (at the request of Henry Fuller Esq.). I was according to appointment at the King's Wharf at 10 o'clock a.m. but in consequence of some repairs the boat required, it was detained until 11 o'clock. Having a head wind with frequent squalls and rain I did not arrive at Chaguanas until 2 p.m. when I immediately proceeded to Felicity Estate. As there were no sick in the hospital, Mr. McChesney furnished me with a mule and I proceeded without a moment's delay to the Edinburgh Estate and delivered the letter for the Manager at the same time requesting him to have all the sick for my inspection on my return from Felicity Hall. I then proceeded to the said estate and on my delivering Mr. McCondon his letter he requested me to walk in and asked me to spend the day with him.

I replied it was absolutely necessary for me to return to town by the same tide and as it was high water at Felicity Hall at 3 p.m. I had only a short time to remain; however another time I would remain longer. Mr. McCondon replied: "You follow Dr. Neilson's plan who always made a wild goose chase visit ". I replied I shall perform my duty and although my passage was unfortunate I have time enough to see all the sick and when I return again I shall bring you a collection of prescriptions that I use on different estates I attend along with a short description for the treatment o/ ordinary cases of disease. lle seemed very well satisfied and accordingly I visited the Hospital, examined Ward carefully and everyone in it. I wrote down the remarks in the manner already submitted to you.

Mr. McCondon took down verbatim my prescriptions, specifying the exact proportion of medicament in each case. My observation respecting the confinement of the people in the stocks were made after we left the Hospital and I merely suggested the propriety of giving those that were in the stocks the indulgence of two hours' exercise daily which is invariably granted even to felons that are undergoing solitary confinement as ulcers occasionally proceed from neglect or design in which case punishment should be inflicted. We are all liable to ulcerated wounds from accident and it must be admitted that whenever punishment is generalised in your hospital with inference either of guilt or innocence it must be illegal, cruel and totally subversive of discipline independent of the effects it must have of expecting the fatal propensity of rigors to despondency which I believe is more fatal to the negroes of Trinidad than all the other disservices they are subjected to.

As to Mr. McCondon's opinion I am perfectly indifferent, or, indeed, the opinion of any man in the performance of so sacred a duty as that of umpire between the respective duties of Master and slave for during the nine years I have practised amongst slaves I had invariably used every exertion to prevent the slaves imposing on their masters (and to which that class are with few exceptions prone) and at the same time whenever a slave was ill-treated I have procured him justice.

As to Mr. McCondon's orders respecting Rosalie I must observe that my motives for recommending her removal to town were as follows:

Rosalie stated to me that the cause of her illness proceeded from a blow she received from a manager to which Mr. McCondon replied that she was a liar and said so because the manager was dead. To make further inquiries (on my part which I considered my duty) in a crowded hospital would be trifling with Mr. McCondon's authority and might prove subversive of that discipline which must be kept up on an estate, and as the unfortunate creature was stretched on the hospital floor without even a dressing on her bed sores emitting a most offensive odour with an overflowing calabash of excrement close to her head and exhibiting a most horrid spectacle of human misery (when such was her state during the day what must be her condition be at night) I considered the most advisable plan to pursue was her immediate removal to town and that after I made further enquiries about the truth of her assertions I might then and not before report facts to you. At all events the unfortunate wretch would have every care she required in her helpless state. The opposition made by Mr. McCondon is, I fear, not dictated by humanity.

As to Mr Robbins I cannot credit Mr. McCondon's assertions regarding him.

Mr Amaro states that Dr. Nielson and myself are both bad.

It is true I took with me my prescription which I submitted to but in his zeal he forgot I presume that Mr. McCondon wrote in my presence the doses of medicine and other advice of mine. Mr. Amaro had upwards of an hour to collect his sick people. I visited Williams in his house and the others in the hospital. It will appear on an investigation that Mr. McCondon and Mr. Amaro are determined to get rid of medical attendance as they fancy it will interfere with their prerogatives and probably afford you too much information respecting the unheard of mortality that prevails on your properties during the last twelve months.

On the different estates I now attend and have attended for upwards of eight years the practice in general in the Colony where a Hospital Book is kept; all the names, admissions and discharges are entered daily by the manager or overseer of the property with the treatment observed and with the nature of the complaint so that when the doctor visits he can at once see the history of the case he prescribes for and either approve or disapprove of same. The regular visits are in my practice once a week except in cases of serious illness so that when a hospital is visited the doctor has only to enter the medical directions above. If the manager is in the fields, reference to the Hospital Book affords him the necessary information and he consequently prescribes the necessary medicine all through the week.

The manager is obliged to administer and prepare the medicines, otherwise it would be impossible for a medical man to attend more than two or three negroes. In the King's service, a medical officer is allowed for 200 men and even then he is allowed a clerk and several servants – one medical man here, I am informed, attends to nearly 3,000 negroes – how could he possibly do his duty if he had to deal with Mr. McCondon or Mr. Amaro? I leave you to judge. As several estates have no Hospital Journal, the manager or proprietor invariably copies down whatever the medical attendant prescribes and sees that his directions are attended to.

ABOUT THE AUTHOR

PHILLIP EMMETT TAAFFE O'CONNOR was born at Arima in 1899. He was educated in Ireland. On leaving school in 1917, he joined the army as an Officer Cadet and on demobilisation in 1919 returned to Trinidad for a short stay during which time he worked in the sugar industry. Returning to the United Kingdom, he obtained a Bachelor of Science degree in Petroleum Mining at the University of Birmingham.

In 1923, he joined the staff of Kern Trinidad Oilfields as the first Trinidadian graduate to enter the local oil industry. Between 1929 and 1937, he saw service abroad with the Shell Oil Company in Egypt, Romania and Argentina.

He returned to Trinidad in 1937 to join Antilles Petroleum Company and was General Manager of that company from 1946 to 1958. From 1958 to 1961, he was General Manager of Premier Consolidated Ltd. He was a Director of Texaco Trinidad Inc.

O'Connor served on various Government boards and was Chairman of the Port Authority from 1962 to 1968.

He was twice elected to the St. Patrick County Council, was a founder member of the South Trinidad Chamber of Commerce and its first President, and twice acted as a Nominated Member of the Legislative Council.

He married Thora, née Brand, and they had six children: five sons and a daughter.

Phillip O'Connor ("Pat") died in 1986.

Printed in Great Britain
by Amazon

37128350R00076